# The Historic Hotels of Paris

## A Select Guide

WENDY ARNOLD

# The Historic
# Hotels of Paris

*A Select Guide*

Photographs by
ROBIN MORRISON

CHRONICLE BOOKS

SAN FRANCISCO

*For Paulina Drew*
*born in San Francisco just before the 1989 earthquake.*
*She slept through it.*

*Frontispiece: the doorman welcomes visitors to the Ritz, now fully restored to its former glory.*

*Opposite: The upper rear windows of the Grand Hôtel look out on to one of the most spectacular of Parisian building – the Opéra – the corner of its façade dominated by the flamboyant figure of Music with her lyre.*

*On p.96: A view across the Champs-Elysées to the Eiffel Tower, from the Crillon Hotel.*

First published in the United States 1990 by Chronicle Books.

Copyright © 1990 by Thames and Hudson Ltd., London.

Printed in Hong Kong

Library of Congress Cataloging-in-Publication Data

Arnold, Wendy.
   The historic hotels of Paris: a select guide/Wendy Arnold; photographs by Robin Morrison.
      p. cm.
      ISBN 0-87701-694-1
      1. Hotels, taverns, etc.—France—Paris—Guide-books.
      2. Paris (France)—Description—1975—Guide-books.
      I. Title.
   TX907.5.F72P372   1990
   647.94443′601—dc20

89–48865
CIP

Cover design by Julie Noyes

Distributed in Canada by
Raincoast Books
112 East Third Avenue
Vancouver, B.C. V5T 1C8

10 9 8 7 6 5 4 3 2 1

Chronicle Books
275 Fifth Street
San Francisco, California 94103

# Contents

# Preface

*The comfortable paneled drawing room of the Pavillon de la Reine.*

Paris is one of the world's most exciting cities. Forty years after my first visit, having been back many times since, I still find it fascinating. The slender, soaring spire of Notre Dame; the Eiffel Tower, which dominates every vista and is unbelievably vast; the Arc de Triomphe, standing so dramatically at the top of the broad, sweeping vista down the Champs-Elysées to the majestic Palace of the Louvre. By night, Paris is doubly magical, with every monument floodlit and the *bateaux-mouches* pleasure boats, glittering as they glide beneath the illuminated bridges of the Seine.

Whether you are going to revisit old haunts and revive old memories or to discover Paris for the first time, it will surprise you. In the heart of the ancient Marais district the Pompidou Center sits like a brightly painted preschool toy; the stone caryatids and lion masks of the Louvre look down in astonishment at the new shining glass pyramid in its courtyard. Walk down a small street on the Left Bank: a wrought-iron gate gives you a glimpse of a hidden garden and an enchanting 18th-century mansion. Look into a shop window: a low-beamed medieval Aladdin's cave of antiques is revealed. Turn a corner: you suddenly find yourself in a colorful street market. After strolling through these varied neighborhoods, what could be better than stopping for afternoon coffee at one of Paris's signature sidewalk cafés? The café, with its tiny tables and ferociously strong coffee, is the center of Parisian society; there you may chat for hours, watch the endless parade of people, or simply spend a leisurely moment in thought. The cafés may whet your appetite for more substantial fare, and Paris, home of the best restaurants in the world, is a gourmet's delight.

Paris hotels are as varied and as memorable as the city itself. The period palaces have been refurbished, revitalized, and regilded; every crystal droplet on their shimmering chandeliers sparkles. They are elegant and sophisticated establishments; they are known for their courteous staffs and skillful chefs. Less overwhelming, and memorably individual, are

the former embassies, ancient convents, and tiny 17th-century timbered houses that have become delightful small hotels.

Having explored France for my book *The Historic Country Hotels of France*, it seemed logical next to investigate the hotels of Paris. I spent a year researching and staying in hotels for each book, arriving unannounced and accepting no fees or hospitality. I discard instantly any hotel where the staff is not polite, welcoming, and efficient. The rooms must be tastefully furnished and well-maintained, the bathrooms immaculate, and the food tempting.

I have never underestimated the immense amount of hard work, dedication, and constant reinvestment needed to keep a hotel up to scratch; sadly, in Paris I found that several former gems had fallen below par. Mark Twain commented on this very phenomenon at the turn of the century in *A Tramp Abroad*: "Now in Europe, the same as in America, when a man has kept an hotel so thoroughly well during a number of years as to give it a great reputation, he has his reward. He can live prosperously on that reputation. He can let his hotel run down to the last degree of shabbiness and yet have it full of people all the time. . . . Its excellent old reputation still keeps its dreary rooms crowded with travellers who would be elsewhere if they had only had some wise friend to warn them."

My aim in writing this book is to be such a friend. I trust that the hotels I have chosen will not disappoint. Should one show signs of allowing its standards to slip, I should be most grateful to hear about it, care of my publishers.

# General Information

**Preparation** Good months to visit Paris are May to early June, and from the end of September until the end of October, especially if you plan to tour France afterwards; seasonal hotels should all be open, holiday traffic, prices, and occupancy below their peak, and the weather at its best. Late July and August in Paris can be hot – most large hotels are airconditioned, but few smaller ones are – and top restaurants close for annual holidays and refurbishment. European weather is unpredictable – I found summer heat in February and frost in June – so always travel with clothes that you can build up in layers, a light raincoat, and an umbrella; also pack walking shoes, as Paris is a wonderful city to walk in. Larger hotels appreciate the formally and fashionably dressed – in some, joggers are asked to use only the back stairs – and most good restaurants expect jackets, ties, and dresses in the evenings.

Book hotels as long in advance as possible, asking them to reserve a table for you at any top restaurants you wish to visit, since same-day or even same-week bookings are usually impossible. Check room details. Twin-bedded rooms are more spacious than those with a double bed. French double beds are romantically narrow, so specify if you want a six-foot king-size. As Paris traffic is noisy, ask for a room high up and facing an inner courtyard; enquire if there is one with a balcony and a view, and check that the elevator reaches it. Book large hotels through an agency, as they can generally get a sizeable discount, especially for weekends, special breaks, or half-board. Small hotels may have tiny bedrooms and little closet space, but their suites are often delightful, spacious, and the same price as a small room in a large hotel.

NB Small hotels do not always take credit cards, seldom have restaurants, and must fill their rooms, so always be sure to confirm your booking, to arrive by *exactly* the time you have stated, and to phone if you are even a little late, or your room will be relet, as I found to my cost. Arrive just after noon to be sure to get the pick of the rooms, and always complain if you are not satisfied. If you travel out of season you will have a better chance of changing rooms if not happy.

Read details in this book carefully when deciding which area of Paris you prefer. On the Right Bank are the most elegant of the hotels, the Louvre, the fashion boutiques of the rue du Faubourg Saint-Honoré and the avenue Montaigne, and the famous night spots; beyond the Louvre is the Marais district with the Pompidou Center, gathering place of the young. The Left Bank offers the Rodin and Orsay museums, hundreds of antique shops, interior designers, smaller boutiques, and ethnic restaurants – and the students of the Sorbonne, who demonstrate from time to time in its medieval streets.

**Terms** Exchange rates fluctuate, so I have divided hotels into four categories, based on the cost of a double room for one night, including tax and service. The approximate sterling and dollar equivalents are based on a rate of 10FF = £1.00 or $1.65.

| | |
|---|---|
| Budget | 490–780FF (£49–78/$81–129) |
| Moderate | 850–1250FF (£85–125/$140–206) |
| Expensive | 1300–1890FF (£130–189/$214–312) |
| Deluxe | 1900FF + (£190+/$313+) |

Note that I have not included breakfast costs – anything from 35FF to 150FF (£3.50–£15.00/$5.70–25) according to the grandeur of the hotel – as this is almost always extra, and you may prefer to go out and eat it in a delightful sidewalk café; drinks and snacks there are also less expensive than hotel room service and minibar. Long-distance phone calls have a high mark-up in big hotels, so enquire how to access your credit phonecard before leaving home. Change money in banks to obtain the best rates.

**Transport** There are plentiful airport cabs, also an excellent Air France bus, though note that this is *not* suitable for those with many bags, or if it is raining, since it deposits you by the kerbside near the Arc de Triomphe, where there is no shelter and often a long wait for a cab. Taxis theoretically form ranks outside big hotels, or at streetside TAXI signs, but vanish during rain, the rush-hour, and at night. They are best obtained by asking hotel, café, or restaurant to phone for one, or by flagging one down, though it will already have a large total on the meter; they also add an extra charge for any bags carried. Drivers are not necessarily familiar with street names, the English language – or even French! A comprehensive subway system, the Metro, covers all Paris, as do buses; hotels will explain their workings. Driving is fast and aggressive. Some hotels have their own garage. City signposting is good, but buy a good map *before* arrival to find your way in from the ring-road, the *périphérique*, and note that many streets are one-way only. For those planning to visit sites outside Paris, I have included one hotel in Versailles with on-site parking and good rail connections with the capital.

**Sightseeing** The Michelin green guide gives details of the principal sights and rates them for interest; I also found a Taride large-scale pocket street atlas with index very helpful – both are obtainable from newsstands. Notes at the end of each hotel entry in this book give details of the main nearby places of interest and good restaurants.

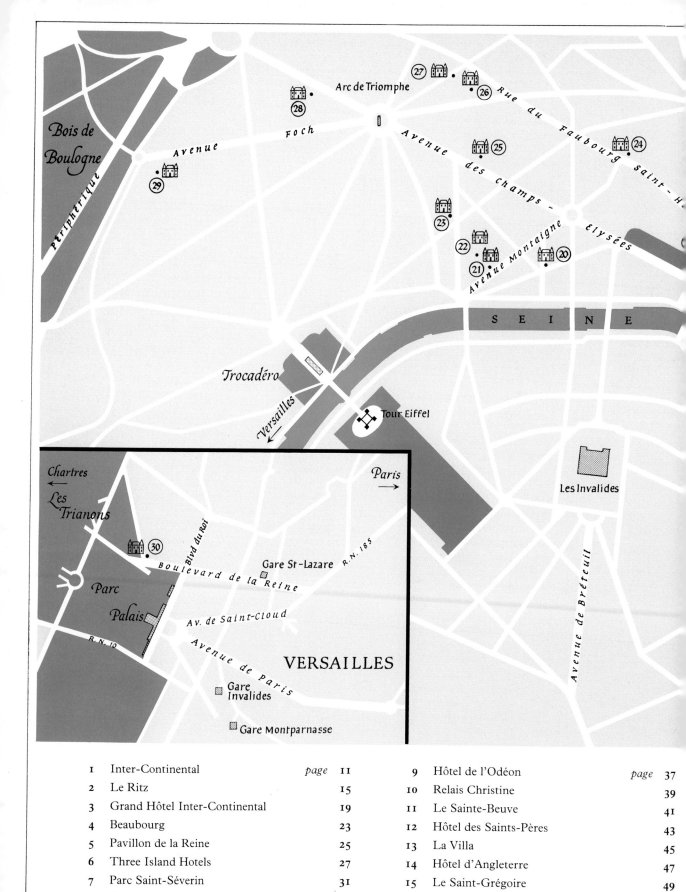

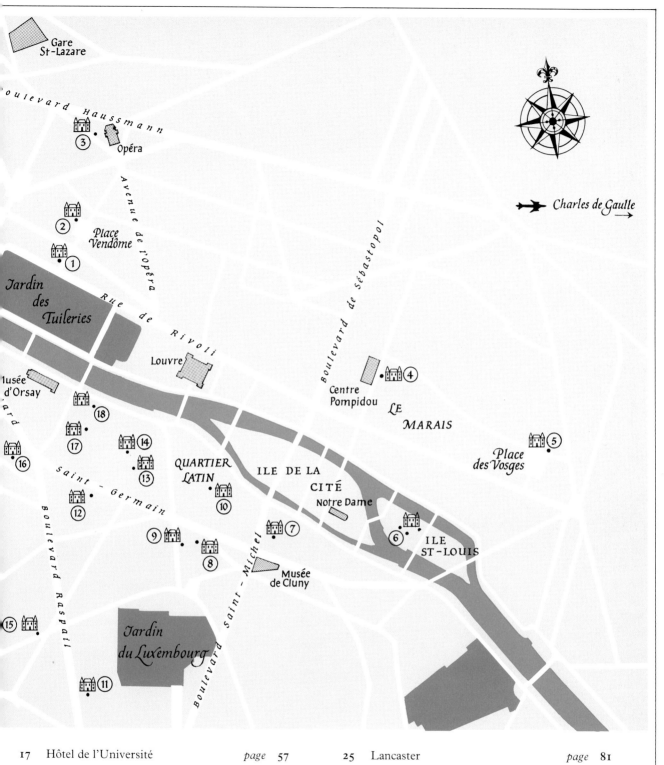

## Overlooking the Tuileries

The Tuileries Gardens, designed by Louis XIV's gardener Le Nôtre, lie between the Palace of the Louvre and the dramatic vista up the Champs-Elysées to the Arc de Triomphe. Overlooking the gardens, on the site of a former Capuchin monastery, is the Inter-Continental, purpose-built as a hotel for the Paris World's Fair of 1878, and designed by the architect Blondel in the style of the similarly ornate and imposing Opera House.

A magnificent pair of giant polished brass candelabra bracket the main entrance, from which shallow steps lead to a vast colonnaded courtyard. In summer, white parasols, cane chairs, and tables with bright blue cloths spill out from the glassed-in Terrasse Fleurie restaurant to surround the courtyard's flower-decked central fountain. In winter, trim tubs of evergreens replace the tables, and guests eat inside in the snug comfort of the intimate Rôtisserie Rivoli, with its rustic decor, starched cloths, gleaming silver, and fresh flowers. Here I enjoyed an excellent meal: a savory shrimp starter – compliments of the chef – followed by a foie gras and green bean salad, a tangy sorbet, tender veal with well-presented vegetables, and succulent chocolate charlotte scattered with fresh raspberries; truffles and petits fours arrived with the coffee. The less formal Café Tuileries is airconditioned and has non-smoking areas; tasty meals are available here throughout the day. Service in all the restaurants is sparkling.

Arriving guests follow a colonnaded arcade round to the right, through the large paneled seating area overlooking the courtyard, which has comfortable chairs divided into conversation groups by pillars and leafy plants. Tempting Parisian designer goods are displayed in showcases near the elevators. The hotel's breathtakingly high-ceilinged original reception rooms, magnificently gilded, painted, and hung with chandeliers, are classed as historic treasures; they are now mainly used for exclusive private receptions, prestigious company presentations, or elegant fashion shows, but deserve a visit if unoccupied. (Ask at reception.)

My bedroom was furnished in pretty fabrics and reproduction furniture with some delightful period prints. The minibar was enterprisingly stocked, offering pâté and authentic Caspian caviar as well as the usual bottles. The bathroom was tiled in green, with well-lit mirrors and a powerful shower; staff tidied the room and changed damp towels whenever I went out. Some rooms have been redecorated in Thirties style, while spacious eaves suites, decorated in warm autumnal tones, have marble bathrooms with jacuzzis, yet to be installed in the formal period suites. Breakfast, smilingly brought on a trolley bearing a rose, had low-calorie options, iced water, and an English-language paper. This hotel provides a welcoming, efficient, and wonderfully historic base from which to explore Paris.

*Opposite: giant polished candelabra bracket the splendid entrance to the Inter-Continental Hotel. Above: one of the snug attic rooms. Overleaf: the glassed-in arcade (right) overlooks the central courtyard (left) in which summer diners can enjoy the elegantly presented dishes.*

HÔTEL INTER-CONTINENTAL, 3 rue de Castiglione, 75001 Paris. **Tel.** (1) 42 60 37 80. **Telex** 220114. **Fax** (1) 42 61 14 03. **Owners** Seibu Saison of Japan/SAS. **Managing Director** Frederik de Roode. **Open** All year. **Rooms** 450 (incl. 16 suites and 54 executive suites), all with bathroom (incl. wall shower), direct-dial phone, TV (incl. in-house videos and satellite English-language channels), radio, minibar, airconditioning, 24-hr. room service, laundry/drycleaning. Some executive suites also with jacuzzi. **Facilities** Sitting room, indoor restaurant September–May, garden restaurant June–September, café/brasserie/bar open daily 6.15 a.m.–2 a.m., 3 elevators, disco Tuesday–Saturday 10 p.m.–dawn, express check-out, newsstand/boutiques in arcade. **Restrictions** Dogs in bedrooms only. **Terms** Deluxe. **Credit cards** All major cards. **Closed parking** Place Vendôme. **Nearest metro** Tuileries/Concorde. **Local eating** Grand Vêfour, Carré des Feuillants, Gérard Besson, Chez Pauline, Pharamond. **Local shopping** Many couturiers, jewelers, boutiques. **Of local interest** Tuileries Gardens; Opera House; The Louvre; Musée d'Orsay; Decorative Arts/Fashion museums; exhibitions at Grand Palais.

## Fit for a prince

The great Paris Ritz was the creation of the doyen of the world's hoteliers, César Ritz, who insisted that his hotel should have "all the refinements of living that a prince might hope to incorporate in his town house." At its opening in June 1898, the Ritz set the highest imaginable standards. Lit by the new electricity, it provided a spacious bathroom for each bedroom, as well as a marble fireplace, Louis XV-style furnishing, wall-to-wall carpets, and walls painted rather than papered, so that everywhere could be kept spotlessly clean and fresh.

"Where Ritz goes, I go," said Edward VII of England, and he came to stay, as did the cream of Europe's high society, who relished the cooking of master-chef Escoffier. To the early 18th-century town house facing the Place Vendôme – once owned by the Duc de Lauzun, who led the French cavalry at Yorktown in 1781 – was added a second property on the rue Cambon, linked by a long gallery of glamorous showcases displaying Paris's most fashionable offerings.

Between the World Wars the Ritz became the meeting place of America's millionaires; but the Thirties' Depression, followed by World War II, began a long decline, ending with the sale of the hotel by the Ritz family in 1979. Thanks to its new owner, Mr. Mohammed al Fayed, the Ritz has been restored to its full glory, at a cost of many millions. Airconditioning, a splendidly elegant basement pool and health club, and a nightclub with a fashionable late-night disco have been discreetly added.

It was at the Ritz that I began my exploration of Paris hotels, and I was delighted to find it fully living up to its august reputation. My rose-pink brocade bedroom had a row of fitted closets, buttons by the bed, and bell-pulls over the tub in the enormous

marble bathroom instantly to summon valet or maid. The peach-colored robe and bath towels were thick and soft, the pillows finest down, the sheets crisply ironed; the bed was turned back while I dined, and a linen mat placed beside it for my feet.

En route to the Hemingway Bar I walked between the 120 showcases filled with the finest luxuries: delicately embroidered table linens, sequined evening wear, exquisite children's clothes, pure silk lingerie, cut-glass flagons of fine perfume – and the glittering wares of Fred the jeweler. I entered the Michelin double-starred Espadon restaurant past a tank of feeler-waving lobsters to enjoy a delicious dinner amid the heavy velvet drapes and palm trees, where an excellent pianist was softly playing, "The Last Time I Saw Paris."

Charmingly staffed, impeccably maintained, hung with tapestries and glittering with chandeliers, its suites vast and magnificent, the Ritz is indeed once again a town house fit for a prince.

*The height of opulence, from the chandelier- and tapestry-hung bedrooms and finely wrought spiraling staircase to the luxuriously paneled bathrooms. The garden courtyard shown left is ornamented by classical statuary (overleaf). Also overleaf: the recently created indoor pool and the Hemingway Bar.*

HÔTEL RITZ, 15 place Vendôme, 75001 Paris. **Tel.** (1) 42 60 38 30. **Telex** 220262 RITZMSC (messages); 670112 RITZRES (reservations). **Fax** (1) 42 86 00 91 (reservations); (1) 42 60 23 71 (messages). **Owners** The Ritz Hotel Ltd. **President** Frank J. Klein. **General Manager** Didier Picquot. **Open** All year. **Rooms** 187 (incl. 46 suites), all with bathroom (incl. wall shower), direct-dial phone, TV, radio, minibar, airconditioning, 24-hr. maid/waiter/valet services, laundry/drycleaning. Some suites with jacuzzi/sauna. Private phone line/fax/telex/video by arrangement. **Facilities** Salon (with afternoon tea), restaurant (open to terrace in summer), 3 bars (1 open to garden in summer), elevators, barber/beauty salon, babysitting, newsstand, car rental (with/without chauffeur), multilingual secretarial services, 5 reception/conference rooms, audio-visual facilities, health club, indoor heated pool, nightclub, late-night disco, Ritz Escoffier Private School of Gastronomy. **Restrictions** None. **Terms** Deluxe. **Credit cards** All major cards. **Closed parking** Place Vendôme. **Nearest metro** Tuileries/Madeleine/Opéra. **Local eating** Grand Vêfour, Carré des Feuillants, Gérard Besson, Chez Pauline, Pharamond. **Local shopping** Many couturiers and jewelers. **Of local interest** Tuileries Gardens; Opera House; The Louvre; Musée d'Orsay.

## Belle-Epoque splendor

The Empress Eugénie approved of the Grand Hôtel when she visited it on the day it was opened, 14 July 1862, just fifteen months and ten days after building began. It was hailed as the most beautiful and comfortable hotel in the world; one of its architects, Charles Garnier, went on to design the equally lavish and flamboyant Opera House which stands opposite. Such grandeur fitted the plans of Napoleon III and Baron Haussmann to ennoble Paris architecturally, and to create wide boulevards, opening the city up to light and air.

Over the years the hotel continued to have great success and a notable clientele – from European royalty to Mata Hari, Offenbach, and Churchill. It was here, in 1869, that Stanley met *New York Herald* owner James Gordon Bennett, who financed his African expedition to find Livingstone. Even today world travelers have their mail sent Poste Restante to its famous Café de la Paix, and rendezvous with friends at its sidewalk tables served by busy waiters from 10 a.m.–1.30 a.m. Artists display their work in the gilded, pillared elegance of the café's airconditioned inner rooms – the Relais Capucines and more formal Michelin-starred Opéra restaurants. I noted many local French customers lunching, a promising sign which was confirmed by sampling the excellent smoked salmon salad, duck, and a light coffee mousse included in the very reasonable menu of the day. The glass-roofed courtyard terrace restaurant serves buffet meals, while the original dining room – lined with mirrors, lit by chandeliers, and with soaring ceilings – now serves as a function room, staffed on State occasions by liveried and bewigged footmen. The foyer is currently being restored to its similar former glory.

The impressively paneled, high-ceilinged and antique-filled main suite (with tiny private kitchen) retains its period charm; other bedrooms have attractive modern decor, and some are duplex. Mine was in shades of soft green, with beechwood furniture, framed architectural prints, brass reading lamps, down pillows, and a modern bathroom. Room service was swift and polished, breakfast ample and good. A gym offers a healthfood bar for those on fitness programs. The hotel's vast size, its wide corridors, efficient elevators, and many well-equipped function rooms, make it convenient for conferences. Individual guests, however, remain pampered; successive generations of the same families return; birthdays are remembered with a card. Every breakfast tray bears a bunch of traditional lily-of-the-valley on 1 May, and gift-wrapped chocolates at Christmas.

Old-world charm and 20th-century efficiency are skillfully blended, so that the Grand, as commended in the 1904 Baedecker Guide, remains a "hotel of the highest class" – though it now charges rather more than the eight francs which was then the tariff per day.

*Opposite: morning – awaiting opening time at the Café de la Paix and (above) a well-appointed bedroom in Thirties style. Overleaf: a splendidly traditional suite; the gleaming interior of the Relais Capucines; the ceiling in a gloriously "belle-époque" reception room.*

GRAND HÔTEL INTER-CONTINENTAL, 2 rue Scribe, 75009 Paris. **Tel.** (1) 42 68 12 13. **Telex** 220 875 GRAND. **Fax** (1) 42 66 12 51. **Owners** Seibu Saison of Japan/SAS. **Managing Director** Frank Mielert. **Open** All year. **Rooms** 515 (incl. 30 suites), all with bathroom (incl. wall shower), direct-dial phone, TV (incl. satellite channels), radio, minibar, airconditioning, room service, laundry/drycleaning. **Facilities** 3 restaurants and 1 café, 2 bars, 3 elevators, gym club with health bar, 20 conference rooms, newsstand, express check-out, babysitting by arrangement. **Restrictions** No dogs in restaurant; small dogs accepted in rooms with charge. **Terms** Expensive. **Credit cards** All major cards. **Closed parking** Rue Caumartin. **Nearest metro** Opéra. **Local eating** Lucas-Carton, Ritz-Espadon, Grand Véfour, Carré des Feuillants, Gérard Besson, Chez Pauline, Pharamond. **Local shopping** Many couturiers, jewelers, boutiques. **Of local interest** The Louvre; Musée d'Orsay; Decorative Arts/Fashion museums; Tuileries Gardens.

## In the heart of the Marais

Unlike London, which never ceases to surprise me by its lack of civilized small establishments charging a sensible amount for a simple room, there are many charming small hotels in Paris. Run by their owners, they have pleasant decor, good bathrooms, are spotlessly clean, and charge reasonable prices. Their rooms are not large; you will probably have to carry up your own bags, use the foyer as a sitting area, and the cellar as a breakfastroom. But with so much to see and do in Paris, and such a variety of wonderful restaurants, you may well favor staying in just such a modest establishment. My challenge has been to sort the good from the once good, since, alas, several – through owners' loss of enthusiasm, or lack of reinvestment and refurbishment – did not live up to their former reputations.

I am pleased to say that I found a visit to the Hôtel Beaubourg a thoroughly happy experience. The beamed entry lobby has a large leather sofa, and one wall is stripped back to its vast medieval limestone building blocks. It was decorated with a big vase of scarlet tulips. I was made welcome by Monsieur Morand, the hotel's owner and a dedicated amateur photographer. A quiet man who is fascinated by, and has studied deeply, the history of the surrounding Marais district, he told me that the house dates from the 1600s, the road from 1207, and that the area has been lived in from at least the 1100s, when the Knights Templar drained what was then a marsh. Madame Morand, smiling and enthusiastic, has designed the harmonious decor of the twenty-eight rooms. The Morands formerly ran a successful brasserie restaurant, but they find that they prefer hotel hours.

Rooms at the front of the hotel have ancient timbered ceilings, some still bearing faint traces of original medieval painted decoration; rooms at the back are totally peaceful, though without beams. One ground-floor bedroom overlooks a tiny courtyard garden; another is more spacious, and opens onto a private light-well terrace. My room had walls covered in peach fabric, toning with a dark green and peach chinoiserie-patterned bedcover. There were attractive pieces of marble-topped rattan and wickerwork furniture, shelved and hanging closets with mirror doors, tall, black ceramic reading lamps, and a well-equipped modern bathroom with gray-flecked tiles, wide marble surfaces, and a hand shower over the tub. Breakfast is served in the rooms, or in the cellar-breakfastroom, which features the original medieval well, now bricked in.

The hotel stands a few yards from the Pompidou Center, in an area which, like London's Covent Garden, has been revitalized, and is much favored by the young. The hotel has attracted a quiet, year-round business clientele, to be seen every morning purposefully setting off with their briefcases for the metro just across the road. The Beaubourg is a pleasant, unassuming, well-run alternative to some of the grander Paris establishments.

*Medieval simplicity greets the arriving guest in two different corners of the reception area (opposite). Above: one of the 17th-century beamed bedrooms.*

HÔTEL BEAUBOURG, 11 rue Simon le Franc, 75004 Paris. **Tel.** (1) 42 74 34 24. **Telex** 216 100. **Fax** (1) 42 78 68 11. **Owners** M. et Mme. Claude Morand. **Open** All year. **Rooms** 28, all with bathroom (incl. hand or wall shower, most also with tub), direct-dial phone, TV, radio, minibar, laundry/drycleaning, safe. Some rooms on ground floor, 1 with terrace. **Facilities** Foyer-sittingroom/bar, cellar-breakfastroom, small glassed-in garden, elevator. **Restrictions** Dogs in bedrooms only. **Terms** Budget. **Credit cards** All major cards. **Closed parking** Under Pompidou Center. **Nearest metro** Rambuteau. **Local eating** Many small local restaurants. **Local shopping** Rue de Rivoli, surrounding pedestrianized area with many small trendy shops. **Of local interest** Pompidou Center with Musée National d'Art Moderne; Ile de la Cité with Notre Dame and Ste.-Chapelle; medieval Ile St.-Louis.

## To a king's design

The Place des Vosges stands on what was once a vast open field, where a huge horse fair was held every Saturday, and at which, it is said, more than two thousand horses changed hands. In medieval times it became the site of the Tournelles Palace, which was pulled down by Catherine de' Medici when her husband Henry II was killed in a tournament in its grounds. It was Henry IV, the *vert galant* – so named for the surprising longevity of his amorous pursuits – who created what was originally called the Place Royale. A Protestant monarch, he healed bitter religious rifts in France by converting to Catholicism, reputedly saying that "Paris was worth a mass." He granted nobles land on which to build houses at their own expense to a unified design, forming a large square with shady arcades, across which the pavilions of the king and the queen faced each other. Completed after his death, the square was inaugurated by a three-day party for ten thousand people celebrating the marriage of the new king Louis XIII. It continued to be a fashionable place to live throughout the 17th century, its gardens frequented by the modish, though when the Court moved to Versailles the area gradually declined. Among the famous who lived here over the centuries were Madame de Sévigny, Cardinal Richelieu, and Victor Hugo, whose house is now a museum.

The square was renamed the Place des Vosges in the 1800s. It is now being restored to its former elegance, the central gardens trimly kept and shaded by neat rows of trees, the arcades lined with fashionable antique shops and galleries, cafés and restaurants, and its façade of white stone, red brick, and gray slate once more immaculate.

Passing through the portal of the lofty Queen's Pavilion into a paved courtyard, you come upon the façade of the Pavillon de la Reine hotel, built in period style by the owner of the Relais Christine hotel on the Left Bank (*see* p. 39), to incorporate genuinely ancient beams, fireplaces, tapestries, and antiques. Each room is different: some are duplex, some are tucked under sloping eaves; all are comfortable, with well-equipped bathrooms and solidly rustic woodwork. The acquisition of medieval surrounding buildings has provided some authentic early rooms, which are well worth requesting. Twin-bedded rooms, as elsewhere, are more spacious than double-bedded. Service, snacks, and breakfast are commendable. There is a paneled drawing room lined with leather armchairs, and an arched cellar, where breakfast is served. Drivers should note that this is one of the rare hotels in Paris to have its very own closed car park.

The arcades enclosing the square and the fascinating medieval streets round about are full of life and good restaurants, though if you want to sample the best you must ask the hotel to book a table for you at least a month in advance. Light sleepers should request a room at the top, but the hotel as a whole is a haven of quiet among busy streets.

*Opposite: entrance to the hotel, leading from the arcaded Place des Vosges, and (above) breakfast waits on a charming canopied four-poster bed.*

PAVILLON DE LA REINE, 28 place des Vosges, 75003 Paris. **Tel.** (1) 42 77 96 40. **Telex** 216 160. **Fax** (1) 42 77 63 06. **Owners** S N C Bertrand. **Manager** S. Sudre. **Open** All year. **Rooms** 53 (incl. 10 duplex and 3 junior suites), all with bathroom (incl. wall shower and hairdrier), direct-dial phone, TV (incl. English-language channel), radio, minibar, room service, laundry/drycleaning. **Facilities** Drawing room, cellar-breakfastroom, courtyard garden, elevator. **Restrictions** None. **Terms** Moderate. **Credit cards** All major cards. **Closed parking** At hotel, free to guests; reserve when booking, as space limited. **Nearest metro** St.-Paul. **Local eating** L'Ambroisie, Ma Bourgogne, Guirlande de Julie, Coconnas, Le Péché Mignon, A Sousceyrac, Benoît, Taverne des Templiers, L'Enclos de Ninon. **Local shopping** Arcades around the Place des Vosges containing small antique shops and art galleries. **Of local interest** Picasso/Carnavalet/Victor Hugo museums; historic Marais district.

# 6 Three Island Hotels

## A world apart

Paris began on the Ile de la Cité as the fortified capital of the Parisii tribe. Conquered by the Romans, it became their settlement of Lutetia. The setting of Notre Dame cathedral and the glorious Sainte-Chapelle, the island is visited by hordes of tourists and remains today very much part of city life. The neighboring Ile Saint-Louis, created in the mid-17th century from two smaller islets and in a wider stretch of the Seine, feels, by contrast, like a world apart, a separate village. Its narrow streets are lined with many useful little shops, as well as fashion boutiques and restaurants.

The Jeu de Paume is the island's most recent hotel, remodeled by architect-owner Guy Prache. This magnificent medieval building, lofty and timbered, was built as an early form of aristocratic tennis court. Passing through a gateway into a quiet cobbled courtyard, you leave the busy street behind and enter the hotel through heavy plate-glass doors. A glass-sided elevator rises up through the massive rafters to a gallery of bedrooms, some duplex, with tightly spiraling iron stairs. (Not ideal for the less athletic or the heavily laden.) More duplex, Provençal-style rooms edge the courtyard. Mme. Prache's decor is uncluttered and cool, with pine, tan leather, plain white drapes, and serene pale marble bathrooms. Modern paintings and antique objets d'art decorate public areas which are floored in handmade tiles.

Traditionalists may prefer the Deux Iles hotel, furnished by its interior-decorator owners M. and Mme. Buffat, with painted rattan furniture, designer fabrics, and well-equipped modern bathrooms with good mirrors and pretty blue-patterned tiles. The

immaculate bedrooms are most attractive, as are those of the Buffats' other hotel just down the street, the Lutèce, which has an impressive stone-flagged hall; both are medieval houses. Twin-bedded rooms are bigger, and inner courtyard rooms quieter, as both hotels overlook the street. It is well worth noting that the owners ask for an arrival time. Estimate generously and phone if you are delayed, since your room will *not* be held after the stated time. Also note that credit cards are not accepted.

In summer the Ile Saint-Louis is thronged with happy holidaymakers until late at night, though the streets are almost deserted if you wake early enough to walk over the footbridge and watch the sun rise over Notre Dame. Out of season the island has a very special quiet magic.

*The Jeu de Paume breakfast area, surrounded by the soaring, ancient timbered building (opposite). Above: the welcoming foyer of the Lutèce Hotel. Overleaf: The Deux Iles Hotel: a prettily tiled bathroom and the comfortable lobby.*

HÔTEL DU JEU DE PAUME, 54 rue St.-Louis en l'Ile, 75004 Paris. **Tel.** (1) 43 26 14 18. **Telex** 205 160. **Fax** (1) 43 26 14 18. **Owner** Guy Prache. **Manager** Elyane Prache. **Open** All year. **Rooms** 32 (incl. 2 suites), all with bathroom (incl. hand or wall shower), direct-dial phone, TV, minibar, laundry/drycleaning. **Facilities** Sittingroom/bar, breakfast area with snacks, 3 cellar-conferencerooms, courtyard garden, elevator. **Restrictions** None. **Terms** Moderate. **Credit cards** All major cards.
HÔTEL DES DEUX ILES, 59 rue St.-Louis en l'Ile, 75004 Paris. **Tel.** (1) 43 26 13 35. **Fax** (1) 43 29 60 25. **Owners** M. and Mme. Buffat. **Open** All year. **Rooms** 17, all with bathroom (incl. wall shower), direct-dial phone, TV, radio. **Facilities** Foyer-sittingroom, cellar-bar (closed August), small glassed-in courtyard garden, elevator. NB No restaurant. **Restrictions** No dogs. **Terms** Budget. **Credit cards** None. NB Travelers checks and currency only.
HÔTEL LUTÈCE, 65 rue St.-Louis en l'Ile, 75004 Paris. **Tel.** (1) 43 26 23 52. **Fax** (1) 43 29 60 25. **Owners** M. and Mme. Buffat. **Open** All year. **Rooms** 23, all with bathroom (incl. wall shower), direct-dial phone, TV. **Facilities** Foyer-sittingroom, elevator. NB No restaurant. **Restrictions** No dogs. **Terms** Budget. **Credit cards** None. NB Travelers checks and currency only. **Closed parking** Beside Notre Dame cathedral. **Nearest metro** Pont Marie. **Local eating** Le Monde des Chimères, L'Orangerie, Le Franc-Pinot, Le Quai des Ormes, Au Gourmet de l'Isle; many small cafés. **Local shopping** Many small boutiques, galleries, etc. **Of local interest** Ile de la Cité with Notre Dame and Ste.-Chapelle; Picasso/Carnavalet/Victor Hugo museums; The Louvre.

## Street of the parchment-sellers

The Hôtel Parc Saint-Séverin is in the heart of the Latin Quarter, looking up the road towards the tree-shaded gardens of the medieval mansion and ruined Roman baths of the Cluny museum, which houses the incomparable rose-pink tapestries of the Lady and the Unicorn. Docile groups of tourists are often to be seen gazing obediently upwards at the ornate façade of the house opposite the hotel, which city guides point out as one of the oldest in Paris. The street on which it stands, the rue de la Parcheminerie, was named after the parchment for documents and book-making sold here in the Middle Ages. The charming little church of Saint-Séverin a few steps away, in which concerts are sometimes held (ask the hotel for details) has its own small leafy garden. Behind the hotel is a maze of narrow lanes, now pedestrianized, which contain many book and print shops: this part of Paris was the happy browsing ground of Hemingway and Joyce.

The hotel has recently been stripped back to its retaining walls, and given a Thirties look inside and out. Spacious, light-filled rooms, with uncluttered lines, color-washed walls, and fitted carpets, contrast with the usually cramped rooms of medieval hotels nearby. The striking foyer has an open seating and breakfasting area in pale gray and white heightened by vivid Pierre Frey designer fabric in rich burgundy. The entire top floor is now one airy suite with a wrap-around balcony and a panoramic view of Paris. Not surprisingly, this suite must be reserved some months in advance, as must the two almost equally attractive bedrooms which form the floor below, and which also have balconies. Other rooms vary in size and shape and are priced accordingly; all are appealing. I found the staff particularly helpful and friendly, and they kept the hotel in pristine condition. In summer months the lower rooms can be noisy, since none is yet airconditioned, though in winter the double-glazing effectively keeps out street sounds. My corner room had windows all round, large leather armchairs, vast closets, a modern bathroom, a touch-dial phone, and remote-control TV. Two steps led up to the bed, on a raised dais, draped with a pure white bedcover. Cool blue modern seascapes, a framed Miró poster, and a ceramic lamp painted with an exotic bird added interest to the decor.

The only problem with this hotel is explaining to taxi drivers how to find it. They must be persuaded to turn off the boulevard Saint-Germain into the rue de Boutebrie, which leads straight to its front door. This achieved, one may apply oneself to exploring the lively and colorful area and choosing from the bewildering selection of tempting small ethnic restaurants. The hotel belongs to the owner of the Hôtel des Saints-Pères (*see* p. 43) and is managed with the same smiling professionalism.

*Champagne to celebrate (above) and Thirties-style elegance and designer fabrics in a spacious bedroom and breakfast area (opposite). Overleaf: early-morning view of the Latin Quarter from the top-floor balcony.*

HÔTEL PARC SAINT-SÉVERIN, 22 rue de la Parcheminerie, 75005 Paris. **Tel.** (I) 43 54 32 17. **Telex** 270 905 OSEVRIN. **Fax** (I) 43 54 70 71. **Owner** Marmont Palvel. **Manager** Victor Lingrand. **Open** All year. **Rooms** 27 (incl. I suite), all with bathroom (incl. hand shower and hairdrier), direct-dial phone, TV, minibar, laundry/dry cleaning. **Facilities** Sitting room, breakfast room, elevator. **Restrictions** No dogs. **Terms** Budget–moderate. **Credit cards** All major cards. **Closed parking** Beside Notre Dame cathedral. **Nearest metro** St.-Michel. **Local eating** Jacques Cagna, Relais Louis XIII, Tour d'Argent, Auberge des Deux Signes, Au Pactole; many small ethnic restaurants. **Local shopping** Book/print/antique shops, boutiques. **Of local interest** Ile de la Cité with Notre Dame and Ste.-Chapelle; Ile St.-Louis; The Louvre; Musée d'Orsay; Musée de Cluny.

## A sophisticated hideaway

The Relais Saint-Germain is a tiny hotel in a medieval house on the lively carrefour de l'Odéon, just off the boulevard Saint-Germain, an area full of sidewalk cafés, good restaurants, and with a nearby street market. Although it has only nine bedrooms and one attic suite with a diminutive balcony looking out over the rooftops, I found it quite the most charming small hotel in Paris. Its owners, the Laipskers, are interior designers, who have not only lavished enormous care and love on every detail of the hotel, but continue to cherish it. With so few rooms, their attentive young managers also have ample time to pamper their guests.

You come in through the stylish green front door to a small foyer with part-mirrored walls. On my visit there was a large vase of vivid yellow chrysanthemums standing on a Louis XV chiffonier with a green marble top, alongside a carved Renaissance lion. Here you are greeted with enthusiasm and interest, and shown up to your room by a valet in neat green stripes. The elevator is minute; the bedrooms – usually only two per floor – are named after famous French literary figures. Mine, "Racine," was twin-bedded, therefore the larger of the two, and, being airconditioned, was a refuge from summer heat and traffic noise alike. It was surprisingly spacious for a medieval room: there was a deep closet with a personal safe; walls were terracotta-colored and hung with fine architectural prints; and bedcovers were in toning designer fabrics with touches of green and blue. There was a large soft sofa, a brown tweedy carpet, and a fascinating mixture of antique and modern furniture. Some striking decorative touches included a handsome Moroccan gilded ceramic pot and a beguiling decoy duck; other rooms contain an 18th-century Provençal writing bureau, a Directoire wine-cooler, silver rose bowls, and a Restoration fruitwood chest of drawers. The bed was firm, with a good reading light, peach blankets, non-allergenic pillows, and crisp sheets. The gleaming triangular bathroom – cleverly designed to fit the irregular contours of the walls – was in white and mottled dark brown marble, with a well-stocked basket of toiletries, robes, well-lit mirrors, and ample ledges. It is always a pleasure to find an efficient shower – mine provided a most satisfactory cascade, very welcome after a day of unseasonal heat.

Breakfast was splendid: delicious pastries and breads, yoghurt, fresh fruit, cheese, freshly squeezed orange juice, and excellent coffee, all included in the room price – only cooked breakfasts are extra. Most guests breakfast in their room, though there is a fascinating cellar arranged as a comfortable seating area and breakfastroom. Part of it was only discovered when the Laipskers pierced a wall, and does not appear on any of the property deeds. Dining out, I luckily avoided the roving bands of students celebrating Mardi Gras by tossing flour and eggs at passersby. (In England we make Shrove Tuesday pancakes instead.) Regaining the calm tranquillity of the hotel, I enjoyed a most peaceful night's sleep, and left feeling that it would be hard to imagine a more delightful hideaway hotel than the Relais Saint-Germain.

*A warm welcome waits in the antique-filled foyer of this bijou hotel (opposite, top). The view above is from the balcony of the rooftop suite (left).*

RELAIS SAINT-GERMAIN, 9 carrefour de l'Odéon, 75006 Paris. **Tel.** (1) 43 29 12 05. **Telex** 201 889. **Fax** (1) 46 33 45 30. **Owners** M. and Mme. Laipsker. **Open** All year. **Rooms** 10 (incl. 1 suite), all with bathroom (incl. wall shower and hairdrier), direct-dial phone, TV, radio, minibar, safe, room-service snacks, laundry/drycleaning. **Facilities** Cellar-breakfastroom/bar, foyer seating area, elevator. **Restrictions** None. **Terms** Moderate. NB Breakfast included. **Credit cards** All major cards. **Closed parking** Rue Lobineau. **Nearest metro** Odéon. **Local eating** Jacques Cagna, Relais Louis XIII, Lapérouse, Le Procope, L'Epicurien; many small cafés. **Local shopping** Antique/print/decorator/book shops, boutiques. NB Owners are interior decorators and can advise where to shop. **Of local interest** Musée de Cluny; Ile de la Cité with Notre Dame and Ste.-Chapelle; Church of St.-Germain-des-Prés.

## Rustic charm on the Left Bank

In the area where the boulevard Saint-Germain crosses the boulevard Saint-Michel there is a dynamic mix of people: students from the nearby Sorbonne, tourists, Parisians – always a great variety of nationalities. The back streets are picturesque, some even verging on the seedy, but they conceal such historic eating places as the Café Procope, founded in 1686, favored haunt of Molière, Racine, and Corneille, Voltaire, Balzac, and Verlaine, and still, judging by the number of people eating there when I tried it out one Sunday lunchtime, doing brisk business in its paneled period rooms. Ask to see the special Sunday menu.

Exploring the area's hotels, I was immediately struck by the charm of the Hôtel de l'Odéon – not to be confused with the rather less alluring Odéon Hotel nearby. Terracotta troughs of bright geraniums were displayed on the window-sills; the tiny entrance hall was a forest of time-warped ancient timbers, interspersed with comfortable chairs and some good pieces of 17th-century rustic furniture, including a handsome carved settle once belonging to a convent. One wall was stripped back to the rough-hewn limestone, and a basket of pink cyclamen stood on a table. The reception desk at the back, beside the hand-adzed beams of the staircase, doubles as a bar, with bottles on display. The small inner hall with simple tables and chairs for breakfasting guests was, I learnt, shortly to have glass doors installed, leading into a newly landscaped, floral patio-garden. I liked the friendly response to my initial enquiries, and returned to stay.

The hotel was built in 1530, and the owners have searched throughout Europe for the interesting pieces of furniture it now contains; the fascinating carved, wrought-iron, or four-poster beds, with heavy lace bedcovers, come from as far apart as Holland, Romania, Spain, and Italy, but look very

much at home. One bedstead features cast-iron figures amid leaves and flowers, while another is inlaid with mother-of-pearl. In summer, request a room on the quiet inner courtyard, since there is no airconditioning. Streetside windows are double-glazed. A second elevator will serve back rooms, which are currently being revamped; all will then have marble-trimmed bathrooms with good showers and hairdriers. There is a simple breakfast, or you can find something more elaborate in a nearby café.

This is not a hotel for those wishing to be pampered, or who travel heavy-laden, as rooms are small, and you may have to carry up your own bags; there are no minibars or robes. A first-time visitor to Paris with little French might prefer a more genteel area and the back-up of a concièrge. The seasoned traveler, however, will enjoy tracking down the ancient buildings of the Cour-du-Commerce-Saint-André, the secret gardens glimpsed everywhere through half-open iron gates, the quaintly carved house-fronts, the little, tree-filled squares and tiny narrow alleyways which make the Left Bank so irresistible.

*The owners combed Europe to find the fascinating pieces that furnish the small bedroom (opposite) and the medieval timbered hall (above).*

HÔTEL DE L'ODÉON, 13 rue Saint-Sulpice, 75006 Paris. **Tel.** (1) 43 25 70 11 **Telex** 206 731. **Owners** M. and Mme. Claude Pilfert. **Manager** Patrick Denis Finet. **Open** All year. **Rooms** 26, all with bathroom (incl. wall shower), direct-dial phone, TV (incl. cable stations), radio. **Facilities** Foyer-sittingroom/breakfastroom/bar, elevator. **Restrictions** None. **Terms** Budget. NB No restaurant. **Credit cards** All major cards. **Closed parking** Beside St.-Sulpice church. **Nearest metro** Odéon. **Local eating** Jacques Cagna, Relais Louis XIII, Lapérouse, L'Epicurien; many small cafés. **Local shopping** Antique/print/decorator/book shops, boutiques. **Of local interest** Ile de la Cité with Notre Dame and Ste.-Chapelle; The Louvre; Musée de Cluny.

## Traditional comfort and monastic calm

Twin bay trees in tubs mark the entrance to the Relais Christine, a 16th-century former convent in the heart of one of the most colorful areas of Paris, just down from the river Seine. Reached through a massive gateway, a cobbled courtyard garden is enclosed on three sides by the gleaming white façade of this august building. Marble steps lead up into a wide entrance hall, with polished floor, fresh flowers in abundance, antique furniture, suits of armor, and a glimpse of a spacious paneled drawing room beyond, where a fire burns brightly in the hearth and big leather armchairs wait invitingly.

When I arrived an attentive porter swiftly appeared to help with my bags, and I was shown up via a small elevator to a beamed attic room, unusually spacious for this part of Paris, with a large, well-equipped marble bathroom. Twin beds had heavy-woven, peasant-style patterned spreads; the walls were covered in dark blue linen, and the fitted carpet was deep gold; there were comfortable velvet armchairs, a table, and a desk in the separate sitting area. My double-glazed windows overlooked the street on one side, the entry courtyard on the other. Some ground-floor rooms lead out into a grassy inner courtyard, and are beamed but small; duplex rooms have massive rustic timber staircases, with larger sitting areas for twin-bedded rooms; most are airconditioned, a great boon in summer months. An extra bonus is the hotel's undergound private parking, free to guests, who should nevertheless reserve a place when booking, as space is limited.

There are magnificent arched cellar-breakfast and conference rooms, the pride of the owner, who has cleverly recreated much of this hotel's atmosphere at his other establishment in the historic Place des Vosges, the Pavillon de la Reine (*see* p. 25), most of

which was custom-built, though it incorporates some truly medieval rooms.

Close by the Relais Christine are fine Michelin-starred restaurants, as well as many small ethnic eating places. Feeling somewhat sated with much dutiful sampling of highly elaborate cuisine, I walked, in the evening, to a nearby tiny Russian café. Sitting at a well-scrubbed wooden table I enjoyed a bowl of peasant-style borsch, ruby-red, filled with assorted vegetables, meat, and of course beetroot, and day-dreamed about a Left-Bank existence in an artist's garret. I then returned through streets filled with people taking the air, reading the menus displayed outside each eating place, or queueing for the cinema just across the street from the gates of the hotel.

The Relais Christine has not been designer-decorated, but its atmosphere is that of a solidly comfortable, pleasantly furnished, traditional quiet retreat, entirely in keeping with its monastic past.

*Opposite: the tranquil courtyard of this former convent and a snug bedroom under the eaves. Above: a corner of the flower-filled hallway.*

---

HÔTEL RELAIS CHRISTINE, 3 rue Christine, 75006 Paris. **Tel.** (1) 43 26 71 80. **Telex** 202 606. **Fax** (1) 43 26 89 38. **Owners** SNC Bertrand & Co. **Managing Director** J.J. Regnault. **Open** All year. **Rooms** 51 (incl. 13 duplex suites), all with bathroom (incl. hand and wall shower), direct-dial phone, TV, radio, minibar, room-service snacks, laundry/dry-cleaning. **Facilities** Drawing room, breakfast room, bar, conference room, inner and outer courtyard gardens, elevator. **Restrictions** None. **Terms** Moderate–expensive. **Credit cards** All major cards. **Closed parking** At hotel, free to guests; reserve when booking room as space limited. **Nearest metro** St.-Michel/Odéon. **Local eating** Jacques Cagna, Relais Louis XIII, Lapérouse, L'Epicurien, L'Arrosée, La Foux, Le Sybarite, Allard; many small ethnic restaurants. **Local shopping** Elegant small boutiques. **Of local interest** Ile de la Cité with Notre Dame and Ste.-Chapelle; The Louvre; Musée de Cluny.

## A fashionable venue

This quietly elegant hotel was created from a tall 18th-century house in a small street off the boulevard Raspail, which runs between Saint-Germain-des-Prés and Montparnasse through the heart of an area beloved of famous writers and artists of the last century and between the wars. With the help of internationally renowned interior designers David Hicks of Paris, a formerly run-down establishment has been completely refurbished, and become a fashionable Paris stopping place favored by many world travelers, who like its laid-back atmosphere.

The impression is that good friends have been called away but have left you their house keys and their obliging staff. Nobody fusses you, but help with booking shows or taxis, and succor in the form of excellent cups of coffee or cocktails, are instantly available. In the hall-sittingroom, where stylish sofas are grouped near the open fireplace, a cheerful fire blazes in the hearth in cooler weather; a small bar and breakfast room are hidden behind the greenery in one corner. Attractive flowers are arranged in the foyer, and a porter helps with bags.

My bedroom was high up among the rooftops – a symphony in white: white bedcover, white table, white blinds at the windows, white closet doors, white bedhead, set off by a pale blue carpet; an ornate, inlaid antique dressing table stood in one corner. The bathroom was tiled in pale gray, with dark gray mottled marble surfaces; a wicker basket of toiletries, a thick, roomy white robe, and big soft white towels were provided. Other bedrooms have a country-house decor with flowered chintzes, so it would be as well to specify which style of room you prefer when booking; all are double-glazed. An excellent breakfast was served on pretty pink- and blue-flowered Royal Doulton china, with a tall pot of coffee and freshly squeezed orange juice.

Although the hotel has no restaurant, there are many close at hand in the nearby boulevard du Montparnasse, including La Coupole, with its Thirties decor, which has preserved a marvelously period atmosphere, with exquisitely courteous and rapid service. Your meal is presented in gleaming silver or copper pans, and served with a flourish in generous portions that have never heard of "nouvelle cuisine." I greatly enjoyed a crisp salad with croûtons and quail eggs, a most authentic eastern curry served with all the appropriate trimmings, including mango chutney, and a splendid Grand Marnier soufflé, presented in its mold and spooned with great artistry on to my plate. It was a pleasure to find such traditional service and cooking.

The old charm of the artists' quarter can still be discovered in this area of wide, tree-lined boulevards, which some may well prefer to the claustrophobically crowded medieval streets closer to the Seine.

*This delightfully relaxed establishment has fashionable David Hicks of Paris decor in the bedrooms (opposite) and stylish lobby (above).*

---

HÔTEL LE SAINTE-BEUVE, 9 rue Sainte-Beuve, 75006 Paris. **Tel.** (1) 45 48 20 07. **Telex** 270 182 STBEUVE F. **Fax** (1) 45 48 67 52. **Owner** Mme. Bobette Compagnon. **Manager** Alain Corbel. **Open** All year. **Rooms** 23, all with bathroom (incl. wall shower), direct-dial phone, TV, minibar, laundry/drycleaning. Some rooms have private terraces. NB 5 suites can be formed from communicating bedrooms. **Facilities** Sittingroom/bar, breakfast room, elevator. NB No restaurant. **Restrictions** Small dogs only. **Terms** Moderate–expensive. **Credit cards** All major cards. **Closed parking** Rue de Rennes. **Nearest metro** Notre Dame des Champs/Vavin. **Local eating** La Coupole, Le Dôme, La Closerie des Lilas, Le Chat Grippé, L'Arpège, Cagouille. **Local shopping** Boutiques, jewelers, shoe shops, couturiers in rue de Grenelle. **Of local interest** Luxembourg Gardens; Tour Montparnasse (view from top); Gobelins Tapestry Workshop; Rodin museum; Postal museum; Les Invalides; twice-weekly market rue Edgar-Quinet.

## A peaceful enclave

One of the great charms of small Paris hotels which have been created from former private mansions is that each forms its own little secret world hidden from the busy streets outside, often with a courtyard garden whose quiet is disturbed only by the twittering of birds. The Hôtel des Saints-Pères is not, as the name suggests, a former monastery – though one stood on this street, from which the hotel takes its name – but was once the luxurious private dwelling of an architect of Louis XIV, and dates from the 17th century.

Plate-glass doors open directly from the street into a stylish modern bar on the left, with well-spaced rattan chairs and a mirrored counter, and past stairs on the right, to the reception desk. This faces the courtyard garden, used in summer for breakfast. In winter or on rainy days, breakfast is served in an attractive inner room with white rattan furniture and pink tablecloths. The girls at the desk are helpful and polite, and there is a porter to carry up bags. Sometimes the manager, a courtly and imposing figure with a fierce white moustache, can be glimpsed, since he regularly visits this and its sister hotel, the Parc Saint-Séverin (*see* p. 31); his advice on sightseeing is worth seeking since he knows this part of Paris well.

Most of the bedrooms are large and look out onto the courtyard; they have commodious hanging closets, and spacious modern bathrooms with good showers, though a notice forbids hand-washing and the use of electric appliances. Some rooms have a rather eclectic mix of furniture; my bedroom, for example, was furnished with basic Thirties originals, and dominated by a large portrait in oils of a periwigged, begowned gentleman with a sensitive and slightly melancholy face. Suites at the back of the hotel are extra quiet, with a pleasant sitting room and large twin bedroom with wicker bedhead and pretty chintz fabrics. Specify your taste in bedrooms when booking.

The pride of the hotel is what must be one of the most original bedrooms in Paris: an amazing vast room one floor up, with a 17th-century gilded, painted ceiling depicting Leda and the Swan attended by a winged Cupid. A large bed is at one end; at the other there is a raised dais with a screen concealing a sunken oval tub with a mirrored surround, other facilities being discreetly hidden in a free-standing closet. Walls are decorated in heavy blue brocade; there is a large antique desk, and a Persian rug on the floor. This room is often, not surprisingly, requested by honeymooners.

Since the hotel is very popular, especially at the height of the tourist season, I had a most frustrating time trying to book a room, without declaring my motives. So always reserve well in advance.

A few steps from the boulevard Saint-Germain with its sidewalk cafés, restaurants, and bustle, this hotel is a peaceful enclave, well removed from the noise of the Paris streets.

*Opposite: above, reception area, opening to a tree-filled courtyard; below, plaque outlining the history of the hotel; and a corner of the garden. Above: a chintzy bedroom.*

HÔTEL DES SAINTS-PÈRES, 65 rue des Saints-Pères, 75006 Paris. **Tel.** (1) 45 44 50 00. **Telex** Sainperotel 204 424. **Fax** (1) 45 44 90 83. **Owner** M. Marmont Palvel. **Manager** Victor Lingrand. **Open** All year. **Rooms** 37 (incl. 3 suites), all with bathroom (incl. wall shower), direct-dial phone, TV, minibar. **Facilities** Sittingroom/bar, breakfast/conference room, courtyard garden, 2 elevators. NB No restaurant. **Restrictions** No dogs. **Terms** Moderate. **Credit cards** All major cards. **Closed parking** Boulevard St.-Germain. **Nearest metro** St.-Germain-des-Prés. **Local eating** Le Divellec, L'Arpège, Ferme-St.-Simon, La Vigneraie, La Marlotte; many small cafés. **Local shopping** Antique/baby shops, furniture, silverware, boutiques. **Of local interest** Churches of St.-Germain-des-Prés and St.-Sulpice; The Louvre; Musée d'Orsay.

## Avant-garde chic

Behind its early 19th-century façade on the rue Jacob lurks the extremely avant-garde interior of La Villa hotel. I must admit that I have not met before with such a radical head-on confrontation of centuries, one which architects from all over Europe have loudly applauded. The specially designed furniture, with its delicate, elongated lines, has been exhibited in the Victoria and Albert Museum in London.

The entrance foyer has a sinuously curving screen, concealing a long bar and breakfast room. The color scheme is a dazzling sharp purple and yellow ochre: stairs descend to what will be a cellar-nightclub. A very high-tech elevator beams you up to the bedrooms, whose originality is startling, since most hotels are either a variation on a country-house theme, chintzy through to stylishly plain, or, especially in Paris, very traditional, with ornate velvet chairs, gilding, mirrors, and chandeliers. Not so La Villa, where room numbers are light-projected onto the corridor carpet. There are dimmer switches, with controls at the door and by the bed, and the striking decor is based in individual rooms on pistachio, burgundy, or peach, with black furniture. A curved bed-head wraps around the very comfortable bed, with circular side tables slotted into it. A desk opens into a vanity table; a coffee table is poised on tall, tapering legs. Indirect lighting is concealed in boat-shapes suspended from the ceiling by mast-like rods; plain gray bedcovers are relieved by bows at the foot. My bathroom was in dark brown marble, with heavily frosted plate-glass surfaces, and off-set controls which sent water cascading down from a concealed faucet into a deep, round, polished chromium wash-handbasin. Towels and robe were thick, soft, and peach-colored. There was an excellent shower – disconcertingly, as I often found in fashionable Paris hotels, un-curtained – and a generous selection of Hermès toiletries. Rooms are medium-sized, so if you

are traveling with a mountain of baggage request a suite.

I must admit to having been tempted by a gloriously sunny morning to rise early and walk down the street to one of those quintessentially Parisian sidewalk cafés where waiters bustle busily about in long aprons and exchange good-natured witticisms with their customers. They were serving heavy white cups of fragrant café au lait, feather-light croissants, rich pain au chocolat, and crusty bread warm from the oven, sliced and buttered in long *tartines*. Refreshed, I walked up to the square in front of the Saint-Germain church, down the rue de l'Abbaye, and back to the hotel via the rue Furstenberg, admiring window displays of exquisite baby clothes, antiques, and designer fabrics.

La Villa is not a hotel about which it is possible to feel neutral. Those who enjoy the innovative, the super-modern and the fashionable will be charmed. Those seeking tradition and antiques should look elsewhere. All, however, will appreciate the hotel's historic setting in the heart of the Saint-Germain-des-Prés district.

*Admirers of ultra-modern design will enjoy the futuristic bathroom (opposite) and avant-garde bar (above) of this strikingly up-to-date hotel.*

HÔTEL LA VILLA, 29 rue Jacob, 75006 Paris. **Tel.** (1) 43 26 60 00. **Telex** 202 437. **Fax** (1) 46 34 63 63. **Owner/Manager** Vincent Darnaud. **Open** All year. **Rooms** 35 (incl. 4 suites), all with bathroom (incl. wall shower), direct-dial phone, TV (incl. satellite English-language channels), radio, minibar, airconditioning/double-glazing. **Facilities** Foyer-sittingroom, 24-hr. bar, elevator. NB No restaurant. **Restrictions** No dogs. **Terms** Budget–expensive. **Credit dit cards** All major cards. **Closed parking** Boulevard St.-Germain. **Nearest metro** St.-Germain-des-Prés. **Local eating** Le Divellec, Ferme-St.-Simon, Bistrot de Paris, Le Petit Laurent, La Calèche, Lipp; many small bistros. **Local shopping** Antique/baby/decorator shops, boutiques. **Of local interest** The Louvre; Musée d'Orsay; Rodin museum.

# 14 Hôtel d'Angleterre

## A historic setting

The Hôtel d'Angleterre is so named because it was once the British Embassy in Paris. It is said that it was here that Benjamin Franklin came to discuss conditions for the Independence of the United States from Britain. Built in 1650, it is a stately building, with an elegant stone façade on the rue Jacob, one of the most charming old streets in Saint-Germain. Past guests at the hotel have included Ernest Hemingway and the famous aviator Charles Lindbergh.

Just round the corner is the cobbled square in front of the ancient Saint-Germain church. This is a favored haunt of street musicians, who arrive with their instruments, tapes, and loud-speakers – I observed a violinist and a flautist – and perform concertos full of complicated trills and arpeggios to the accompaniment of a full orchestra, thanks to specially made backing tapes. Their strategically placed hats and instrument cases are soon filled with coins by an appreciative crowd of passing tourists. This square, like the side streets and the wide boulevard Saint-Germain, is lined with restaurants and bistros. Sample the well-known cafés, Flore, Lipp, and the Deux Magots. There is a marvelous street market nearby in the rue de Seine, selling flowers, cheeses, sausages, pies, vegetables, fruit, and many tempting prepared hors d'oeuvres, with colorful vendors who keep up a stream of amusing *badinage* with the shoppers.

In keeping with its former status, the Hôtel d'Angleterre offers a restrained welcome. It has a well-tended courtyard garden, overlooked by a discreet small bar, from which you may stroll in summer to sip your drink under a parasol amid the flowers. For less clement weather there is a comfortable and distinguished drawing room. This is reached through the breakfast room, immediately to your right on entering. With its grand piano and impressive chandelier, it has something of the air of a gentleman's club – the perfect place to read the morning paper.

As in most small Paris hotels, each bedroom is different: facing you as you enter on ground level at the back of the courtyard is a spacious beamed room much favored as cool and shady in summer, while the one directly above is much requested in winter, since it is brighter; both are decorated in floral designer fabrics and have impeccable modern bathrooms. Courtyard rooms are quiet, and I was pleased to find that my small eyrie up under the eaves looked into the garden, and was cool in the hot weather. It had a pleasant decor of greens and browns, a beamed ceiling, and was reached either by elevator or via a gracefully curving staircase whose walls are painted to resemble marble. Work was then in progress to convert a nearby attic room into a small suite – but all rooms will by now have been redecorated. When booking you may wish to request one of the rooms which has a marble bathroom and overlooks the courtyard, though the hotel will not usually promise a specific room number. The staff are pleasant and quietly helpful: this is a hotel well suited to those seeking dignified and traditional surroundings.

*The inner courtyard (left) – a quiet haven of peace from the busy street outside (above).*

---

HÔTEL D'ANGLETERRE, 44 rue Jacob, 75006 Paris. **Tel.** (1) 42 60 34 72. **Fax** (1) 42 60 16 93. **Owners** Private society. **Manager** Mme. Soumier. **Open** All year. **Rooms** 29 (incl. 1 suite), all with bathroom (most with wall shower), direct-dial phone, TV, laundry/drycleaning. **Facilities** Drawing room, breakfast room, bar, courtyard garden, elevator. NB No restaurant. **Restrictions** No dogs. **Terms** Budget-moderate. **Credit cards** Amex/Diners/Visa. **Closed parking** Boulevard St.-Germain. **Nearest metro** St.-Germain-des-Prés. **Local eating** Le Divellec, Ferme-St.-Simon, Bistrot de Paris, Le Petit Laurent, La Calèche; many small restaurants. **Local shopping** Antique/decorator/baby shops, boutiques. **Of local interest** The Louvre; Musée d'Orsay; Rodin museum.

## *Welcoming elegance*

Following the launch of the Hôtel le Sainte-Beuve (*see* p. 41), another hotel, also decorated by David Hicks of Paris, has been created in much the same genre by different owners, in a charming late 18th-century house in the rue de l'Abbé Grégoire. With François de Bene as manager, it has the low-key, modishly relaxed and stylish manner which sophisticated travelers enjoy; the Saint-Grégoire hotel has been an instant success.

It has an added bonus: owners Lucie Agaud and her associate Michel Bouvier also own the delightful little medieval restaurant "La Marlotte" just round the corner in the rue du Cherche-Midi. Here hotel guests are warmly welcomed and instantly feel part of the neighborhood; they dine beneath medieval beams, seated on traditional velvet benches down both sides of the room, with small square tables drawn up in front of them and candles lit at night. At the back is a more open area with larger round tables. A fine collection of antique dishes and keys hangs on the walls; there is a short hand-written menu of delicious food, and a marvelous atmosphere. Light meals and snacks can also be served, by arrangement, at the hotel.

Several of the rooms at the hotel have their own private terrace or diminutive garden, with table and chairs, where you can retire in the evening to sit in plant-decked quiet – these are at the back of the hotel. If you decide not to eat out, this is a pleasant place to enjoy a glass of wine and a salad; in the morning you can breakfast in comfort. An awning pulls down to shade you from the sun, and to ensure your privacy.

Arriving at the hotel, I walked into the large reception room, to be cordially greeted by manager François; he was sitting behind a large antique desk on the left, on which lay a shallow wicker basket full of perfumed white hyacinths. There was a welcoming

fire in the hearth on the right, surrounded by sofas, and a tiny bar beside a minute glassed-in garden; steps led down to the cellar-breakfastroom, where tables were set out with starched white cloths. My room had deep pink walls half-paneled in white, with peachy-pink toning designer fabric at the windows, and a serenely plain marble bathroom with robe and shower. A framed 19th-century print of an idealized child, an antique glass lamp, a bunch of delicate pink tulips, and some glossy walnut-veneered period furniture had been added by owner Lucie Agaud, who delights in tracking down interesting antiques to embellish bedrooms, and is often on hand to chat with guests. Breakfast is brought by girls in neat blue uniforms with crisp white aprons, and is excellent.

The enthusiasm of the owners for their much-cherished hotel, and the relaxed calm of its management style make the Hôtel Saint-Grégoire a most particularly pleasant Paris hideaway.

*The owners have added interesting personal touches to the designer decor of this hotel. Overleaf: as in many of the historic small hotels there is an impressive stone cellar-breakfastroom.*

---

HÔTEL LE SAINT-GRÉGOIRE, 43 rue de l'Abbé Grégoire, 75006 Paris. **Tel.** (1) 45 48 23 23. **Telex** 205 343. **Fax** (1) 45 48 33 95. **Owners** Lucie Agaud and Michel Bouvier. **Manager** François de Bene. **Open** All year. **Rooms** 20, all, with bathroom (incl. hand shower and hairdrier), direct-dial phone, TV, radio, laundry/drycleaning. NB Airconditioned room on 6th floor, 2 ground-floor rooms have small gardens, other upper rooms have small terraces. **Facilities** Sittingroom/bar, breakfast room, tiny glassed-in garden, elevator. **Restrictions** None. **Terms** Moderate. **Credit cards** All major cards. **Closed parking** Rue de Rennes. **Nearest metro** St.-Placide. **Local eating** La Marlotte, La Coupole, Le Dôme, L'Arpège. **Local shopping** Antique/shoe shops, jewelers. **Of local interest** Luxembourg Gardens; Rodin museum; Tour Montparnasse (view from top); Gobelins Tapestry Workshop; Postal museum.

## *Leafy calm in the city's heart*

I enjoyed staying at the Duc de Saint-Simon; the entrance courtyard full of flowers, the comfortable antique-filled drawing room, and the peaceful night I spent there – as tranquil as if I had been in the heart of the countryside. My bedroom windows opened into an enclosed, tree-filled garden; it was raining, and the only sound I could hear was the rain pattering on the leaves. The room was filled with the marvelous smell of rain-washed greenery. Its walls and the spaces between the low beams were papered in a tiny blue flower pattern. There was a matching bedcover, silky-soft sea-island cotton sheets with the hotel's initials embroidered on them in blue, and large, square, down pillows; on the walls were hung period prints of bewigged gentry playing at being rustics, and an oversize mirror in an impressive gilded frame. My bathroom had dusky-pink handmade tiles, a shower stall as well as a tub with a hand shower, and a basket of toiletries. Very useful touring information was provided on the desk. There was no TV, since this is supplied only on request. Would-be guests should also note that only travelers checks and cash are accepted by the hotel – no personal checks or credit cards – though there are banks nearby.

The owner, Mr. Lindquist, is Swedish, kind, precise, and cosmopolitan; originally an executive from the automobile industry, he joined Inter-Continental hotels, launching their Cologne hotel, but is now delighted to have acquired his own small *hôtel de charme*. When I met him just as I was leaving, I found that he still travels widely, so we were able to exchange information on favourite haunts with all the enthusiasm of collectors swapping stamps.

The hotel had been very run-down when it was first purchased, but has now been totally refurbished. Each room is different: one has a Napoleonic-style bed and hand-painted, *trompe-l'oeil* doors. The present building dates mainly from the early 19th century,

though some walls remain from the original 18th-century convent that once stood here, and its cellars have been enlarged to form an attractive sitting room and convivial bar.

Room-service snacks are good; pea and ham soup arrived in a silver tureen, and an asparagus quiche was excellent. I lunched next day just down the road at the Michelin-starred Ferme-Saint-Simon, and enjoyed an artichoke heart and foie gras salad, a splendid dish of sole arranged in the shape of an Indian turban, swathed over fresh noodles and bejeweled with emerald-green broccoli and shellfish, followed by a dessert of white and bitter chocolate – everything tasted as good as it looked.

The street is named after the literary duke who lived in the neighborhood in the 17th century, and whose history is told in a small book obtainable from the hotel. Many of the mansions he would have known still exist, as embassies or government ministries, though the streets are quieter now than when the carts went rumbling down the nearby rue du Bac, laden with goods to be ferried over the river to the still unfinished Palace of the Louvre.

*A comfortable and peaceful pied-à-terre with snug bedrooms and (overleaf) a tranquil garden.*

DUC DE SAINT-SIMON, 14 rue de Saint-Simon, 75007 Paris. **Tel.** (1) 45 48 35 66. **Telex** 203 277. **Fax** (1) 45 48 68 25. **Owner** G. Lindquist. **Manager** Mme. K. Lalisse. **Open** All year. **Rooms** 34 (incl. 5 suites), all with bathroom (incl. wall shower), direct-dial phone. NB TV by request only (extra charge), room-service meals (also from Ferme-St.-Simon by arrangement), laundry/drycleaning. 4 rooms with terraces, some ground-floor rooms. **Facilities** Drawing room, cellar-bar, small outer courtyard/garden, inner garden without access, elevator. NB No restaurant. **Restrictions** No dogs or other pets. **Terms** Moderate–expensive. **Credit cards** NB No credit cards or personal checks accepted. **Closed parking** Boulevard Raspail. **Nearest metro** Rue du Bac. **Local eating** La Ferme-St.-Simon, Le Télégraphe, Bistrot de Paris. **Local shopping** Antique/baby/decorator/shops, boutiques. **Of local interest** The Louvre; Musée d'Orsay; Rodin museum.

## *An antique-collector's haven*

You will not find the name of this hotel on any eye-catching sign, but carved discreetly into the stone above the door, since the rue de l'Université is part of the protected historic district that surrounds the church of Saint-Germain-des-Prés, itself once part of a fortified and moated Benedictine monastery. Built in the 6th century amid vast acres of gardens and fields, and the burial place of the Merovingian kings, the church was twice destroyed by the Normans, before being finally rebuilt in the 11th century. The abbey was dissolved during the Revolution, and of the fields, or *prés*, among which it stood, only the tiny garden behind the church, and the name, remain.

The Hôtel de l'Université is built of massive blocks of stone, and the foyer displays vast ancient timbers, with a small reception desk tucked among them on the left, beside a seating area with well-worn leather armchairs. A small, glassed-in garden faces the door, and a most elegantly curving staircase leads upwards into a paneled stairwell on the right. The greeting is quietly friendly, and one of the tidily aproned middle-aged ladies who form the staff helps with the luggage.

There is a small elevator, serving all but the very top floor, which is reached up a further short, steep flight of stairs, and contains two rooms. One double room has a brass bedstead; the other twin room is larger, with a tall, baroque eastern dressing table and a small dressing or child's room attached. Both have balconies with table and chairs set out for a sun-lit breakfast high up above the streets. On the floor below a spacious room at the back looking over a quiet courtyard contains some fine 17th-century carved oak furniture. There are some simple but reasonable rooms with shower only – the one I stayed in was tucked under the eaves and perfectly comfortable – though the larger bedrooms with fully equipped modern bathrooms are probably to be preferred.

Note that no credit cards or personal checks are accepted.

Most of the carpets throughout are a deep gold color that sets off well the fine antiques in the attractively decorated bedrooms. The special charm of this traditional hotel, however, is that the remarkable collection of furniture is there for use and the practical storage of clothes, and not as part of some rather pretentious designer decor. There is a fine cellar-bar, with a vaulted ceiling, believed to have been a Knights Templar chapel; this leads into a further, barrel-roofed cellar once used as an ice-house for the Louvre Palace. Both are full of fascinating antiques, and provide a congenial setting for a quiet evening.

As it lies on the edge of the famous Carré des Antiquaires, within easy walking distance of more than 125 splendid antique shops, it is not surprising to find that many of the faithful guests of this agreeable hotel are dedicated antique-collectors.

*An antique-lover's paradise in a charming old house in the Carré des Antiquaires. Opposite: the graceful staircase, tiny inner garden, and a comfortable bedroom. Above: the cellar, an Aladdin's cave of treasures.*

HÔTEL DE L'UNIVERSITÉ, 22 rue de l'Université, 75007 Paris. **Tel.** (1) 42 61 09 39/42 61 49 58. **Telex** 260 717 OREM 310. **Fax** (1) 46 64 00 80. **Owner** Private society. **Manager** Mme. O. H. Bergmann. **Open** All year. **Rooms** 28, all with bathroom (incl. wall shower, some without tub), direct-dial phone, TV, some with minibar, room-service snacks, laundry/drycleaning. 2 top rooms have terraces. **Facilities** Sitting area, cellar-bar, small glassed-in courtyard garden, elevator. NB No restaurant. **Restrictions** None. **Terms** Budget–moderate. **Credit cards** NB No credit cards or personal checks accepted. **Closed parking** Rue du Bac. **Nearest metro** St.-Germain-des-Prés/Rue du Bac. **Local eating** La Ferme-St.-Simon, Le Divellec, L'Arpège, Récamier, Le Petit Laurent, Bistrot de Paris, La Calèche; many small local restaurants. **Local shopping** Antique shops, also baby/print/furnishing shops, boutiques. **Of local interest** The Louvre (over footbridge); Musée d'Orsay; Rodin museum.

## Close by the museums

I have lost count of the number of small hotels I looked at in Paris; it must be a hundred or more. Most of them, though perfectly adequate for a night's stay and reasonably priced, lacked that extra something: a friendly greeting, a tasteful, gleaming foyer, individual furnishings – in short, personality. Having visited the Musée d'Orsay, I walked down to look at the Bersoly's hotel, and liked it. My first attempt to stay was defeated by workmen in the road outside chopping through the waterpipe supplying my intended room on the morning of my arrival. The owner had considerately – though she did not realize how frustratingly – booked me in elsewhere. I persevered, and, returning on a subsequent visit, finally achieved a small double room at the back of the hotel, looking out into a light-well, and very peaceful.

The walls were lined with dark red linen; the bedcover was in toning wavy stripes of red and pink. There was a desk, a TV high on the wall in a corner, well-placed brass reading lamps, a plump, red velvet chair, fitted carpet, and a tiny, immaculate, ultra-modern bathroom with red-tiled floor, a shower, and hairdrier. The twin rooms at the front are larger, lighter, and have bigger bathrooms including tubs. All rooms are double-glazed; each has its own special decor; all are attractive. The topmost room is larger than the others; the lowest has a tiny terrace garden in the light-well, and there is a minute cellar-breakfast-room. The beamed foyer and the timbered stairwell, as well as the ceiling rafters in the bedrooms, are all original and date from the late 17th century.

The Bersoly's hotel stands in the very heart of the renowned Carré des Antiquaires, a small block of streets in which virtually every shop is an antique shop. At the end of May each year there is a five-day antiques fair, during which local antiquarians put on display in their windows their discovery of the year: just one especially rare, valuable, or beautiful object.

People from all over the world attend the fair, exchange information, and buy antiques.

Not all guests at the Bersoly's hotel are antique-hunters, however. Many come to see the new Musée d'Orsay, whose collection of paintings, sculpture, furniture, and photography from 1848 to 1905, imaginatively displayed in this very grand former railway station, complements the more contemporary art in the Pompidou Center. Visitors should not miss the wealth of Impressionists and Post-Impressionists in the upper gallery or the experience of eating even a quick buffet meal in the magnificently ornate restaurant. Remembering the usual grim museum eating places, which so often are like school canteens, serving similar food, I looked into the restaurant without enthusiasm, and was dazzled to find it full of chandeliers, mirrors, and gilded statuary under a lofty ceiling. Waiters in long aprons serve you with brisk *bonhomie*, and you may make a rapid meal from an excellent cold table, or linger over more elaborate hot dishes.

You have only to walk down to the river Seine and across the Pont des Arts footbridge to reach the Louvre – this hotel is ideal for the art lover.

*Small, comfortable corner of the cellar and (above) Cookie, one of the owner's two delightfully well-behaved dogs.*

BERSOLY'S SAINT-GERMAIN, 28 rue de Lille, 75007 Paris. **Tel.** (1) 49 60 73 79. **Telex** 217 505. **Fax** (1) 49 27 05 55. **Owner/Manager** Mme. Carbonnaux. **Open** All year except 15–28 August. **Rooms** 16 (larger one at top of house, ground-floor room with small terrace), all with bathroom (incl. wall shower), direct-dial phone, TV, radio, room-service snacks, laundry/drycleaning. **Facilities** Foyer-sitting area, cellar-breakfastroom/bar. NB No restaurant. **Restrictions** None. **Terms** Budget. **Credit cards** Visa/Access/Euro-card/Mastercard. **Closed parking** Rue du Bac. **Nearest metro** Rue du Bac/St.-Germain-des-Prés. **Local eating** Ferme-St.-Simon, Bistrot de Paris, La Calèche, Le Télégraphe, Le Voltaire. **Local shopping** Antique/baby/print/decorator shops. **Of local interest** The Louvre; Musée d'Orsay; Rodin museum.

## Gilded magnificence

Leaving after an enjoyable stay at the Crillon, having asked to see the manager, I presumed that the young man coming towards me across the foyer's shining marble vastness would usher me up to some august hidden presence. I was astonished to find that this was the manager himself. Hervé Houdre – modest, unpompous, sparkling with ideas and enthusiasm – is totally unperturbed by the challenge of running the last of the great palace hotels in Paris still to be in French hands, greeting everyone – from doorman to visiting ambassador – with the same unruffled friendliness.

Commissioned by Louis XV in 1758 and designed by the famous architect Jacques-Ange Gabriel, the property of the Counts of Crillon until 1907 and now in the care of the Louvre Society, under the auspices of the Taittinger family's champagne house, the Hôtel de Crillon is an architectural gem. Its classical pillared façade overlooks the Place de la Concorde, beside the American Embassy, and its magnificent, marble-clad interior is embellished with fine plasterwork and gilding. Public rooms, which are dazzling, include a vast glittering foyer and an impressive main salon overlooking a superb 18th-century courtyard, in which you may sit under striped parasols in summer. There is a series of high-ceilinged reception rooms which can become an apartment fit for a king or head of state.

The Ambassadeurs restaurant, which has won two Michelin stars, is a chandelier-hung masterpiece, lined with mirrored doors through which waiters appear and disappear disconcertingly like Alice through her looking glass, among cascades of flowers worthy of the Chelsea flower show. It also serves some of the best food in Paris. Open the menu and everything sounds tempting; food arrives looking exquisite and tasting wonderful. Salmon tartare is garnished with both vivid red and pearly gray caviare;

stuffed freshwater crayfish have a hint of fennel; a chilled peach soufflé is ringed with a darker apricot coulis and tiny golden melon balls, and trimmed with a gossamer-light, crispy pâtisserie butterfly; petits fours served with the coffee melt in the mouth. And this was just my selection from the extremely good value business lunch. Serious gourmets can invest in a multiple-choice feast. A second restaurant, the Obélisque, with Lalique chandeliers and Baccarat crystal, has the atmosphere of a club, and brisk, excellent service. Food is delicious.

Bedrooms have classically plain-painted, paneled walls; bedcovers and drapes are mainly of rich, heavy, unfigured wild silk or satin; bathrooms are modern and marble, and there is soundproofing and airconditioning. Some suites have balconies overlooking the Place de la Concorde, and one includes a fine hand-painted room – once a private chapel; all are well-equipped. Breakfast is excellent. A friendly welcome, polished formal service, an imposing building, and superb food make the Crillon an outstanding hotel.

*Elegance reigns in the drawing room (opposite), decorated by Sonia Rykiel, and in the Salon des Aigles, with its magnificent ceiling (above). At night the stately façade lights up the Place de la Concorde (overleaf) while the Salon des Ambassadeurs restaurant glitters for its fortunate guests. Further relaxation can be found in the polished marble foyer and the convivial bar.*

HÔTEL DE CRILLON, 10 place de la Concorde, 75008 Paris. **Tel.** (1) 42 65 24 24. **Telex** 290 204 (reservations); 290 241 (messages). **Fax** (1) 47 42 72 10. **Owners** Société des Hôtels Concorde. **Managing Director** Jean Taittinger. **General Manager** Hervé Houdre. **Open** All year. **Rooms** 190 (incl. 27 suites), all with bathroom (incl. wall shower), direct-dial phone, TV (incl. cable with BBC1/CNN/RAI/RTL/ZDF, children's Canal J, MTV, Sports), radio (incl. BBC), minibar, 24-hr. room service, same-day laundry/drycleaning. **Facilities** Main drawing room, 2 restaurants/ summer outside dining in courtyard, 2 bars, 7 private reception/conference rooms, 3 elevators. **Restrictions** None. **Terms** Deluxe. **Credit cards** All major cards. **Closed parking** Under Place de la Concorde. **Nearest metro** Concorde. **Local eating** Laurent, Lucas-Carton, Ledoyen, Pavillon de l'Elysée. **Local shopping** Rue du Faubourg St.-Honoré boutiques. **Of local interest** Musée d'Orsay; The Louvre; exhibitions at Grand Palais; Tuileries Gardens.

## A civilized pied-à-terre

Most of the guests who stay at the San Régis regard it as their private Paris club. The diminutive yet elegant marble reception area includes a tiny salon where you can wait in civilized comfort for the arrival of a friend or taxi. The marble stairs lead up and then down again into what, more than any other small Paris hotel, feels like somebody's tastefully furnished private house. This probably results from the pleasantly eclectic mix of 17th- and 18th-century furniture, combined with comfortable chintz-covered sofas, modern reading lamps, and fine pieces of Chinese porcelain. An open fire burns welcomingly; magnificent carved paneling lines the broad hallway; a small, glassed-in garden full of flowers adds a splash of color to the restful decor. The atmosphere of this mid-19th-century house is tranquil; seating areas are well separated to allow private conversation. There is a raised dais in one corner with a mirrored modern bar set under a dark green ceiling among pillars which lead into the dining area.

Here the peach walls are patterned in foliage, whose dominant tones are echoed in the terracotta, blue- and jade-striped seats of the stylish dining chairs. There are paintings of flowers and fruit by Boucher, Morain, and Sureau, and delicate porcelain is displayed in a recess. Overhead and on the walls are an unusual chandelier and sconces of green-painted wrought iron, with curving tendrils and blossoms, which were specially commissioned. From a simple menu I chose freshly sliced Parma ham, chicken Florentine in a light sauce with excellent spinach and baby carrots, and a self-indulgent gâteau made with fresh raspberries and cream. Petits fours accompanied the coffee – it was all expertly cooked, and attentively and smilingly served.

At each end of the wide hallway a small staircase with solid oak banisters leads up to the bedrooms – there is also an elevator. A few rooms are conventionally formal with crystal chandeliers and imposing antique furniture. Most, however, have a harmonious blend of modern and antique, and striking matching drapes and bedcovers. One duplex suite high up under the eaves has a balcony with a view over rooftops to the Eiffel Tower. Many of the rooms are very spacious, and all have well-equipped bathrooms. You should state your preferred style of furnishing when booking. My room, though small, pleased me, with its soft dove-gray walls, and a bedcover patterned in large, pale pink tulips.

The unobtrusive and polished service is overseen by Monsieur Georges. Even the most demanding of international travelers will find the San Régis a delight.

*A canopied entrance (above) welcomes you to a tastefully furnished hotel with a small restaurant (opposite, top) which serves delicious light meals. The staircase (left) leads up to spacious bedrooms. Bathrooms (far left) are well-equipped and attractive. Overleaf: restful drawing room; one of the large, handsome bedrooms; the intimate bar.*

HÔTEL SAN RÉGIS, 12 rue Jean Goujon, 75008 Paris. **Tel.** (1) 43 59 41 90. **Telex** 643 637. **Fax** (1) 45 61 05 48. **Owners** Société Hôtelière et Touristique San Régis. **Manager** Maurice Georges. **Open** All year. **Rooms** 47 (incl. 14 suites), all with bathroom (incl. wall shower and hairdrier), direct-dial phone, TV (incl. satellite channels), radio, minibar, room service, laundry/drycleaning. **Facilities** Drawing room, restaurant, bar, small glassed-in garden, elevator. **Restrictions** No dogs. **Terms** Expensive-deluxe. **Credit cards** All major cards. **Closed parking** Rue François Ier. **Nearest metro** Franklin D. Roosevelt/Champs-Elysées Clemenceau. **Local eating** Ledoyen, Lasserre, Taillevent, Ramponneau, Duquesnoy. **Local shopping** Avenue Montaigne high-fashion luxury boutiques. **Of local interest** Exhibitions at Grand Palais; Palais de la Découverte; Eiffel Tower; River Seine tours on *bateaux-mouches*; Les Invalides; The Louvre; Musée d'Orsay.

## Palatial luxury

The great palace hotels are the pride of Paris, and one of the grandest, first created in 1867 as the Hôtel Athénée, then re-created in 1911 as the Plaza Athénée, stands on what is now the most fashionable street in Paris, the avenue Montaigne. This angles off from the mid-point of the Champs-Elysées, dividing commercial bustle from the tree-lined walks that lead down to the Place de la Concorde. The boutiques of the most elegant couturiers, jewelers, and parfumiers of Paris are on the avenue Montaigne, and their owners and distinguished clientele, together with visiting film stars, royalty, and all the *beau monde* of Europe gather in the Plaza Athénée's Relais Plaza grill room, to see and be seen, to browse through a short menu of delicious, light Italian and French dishes, sip cocktails or coffee, gossip and relax.

The exterior of the Plaza Athénée is covered in rounded wrought-iron balconies with stone balustrades and scarlet shades, and is bright with flowers and greenery. The inner courtyard, where creeper-clad walls resound with the twitter of birds, is filled in summer with tables shaded by scarlet parasols. Picking my way through the parked Rolls Royces, I entered the impressive foyer – a graceful pillared oval fragrant with flowers, draped in brocade, and featuring specially made Sèvres sconces. This is the domain of the *huissier*, with his silver chain, who greets arriving guests as to a royal residence.

I was shown to my room by a black-jacketed and courteous young man, who checked that I approved it, offered further assistance, and then vanished, succeeded by a porter bearing my bags. Bellpushes instantly produced valet or maid, smiling and helpful; room-service orders were rapidly brought and conveniently served on a damask-covered trolley-table. The bedrooms are lavish – mine was paneled in pale cream brocade, with vast fitted closets and a spacious marble bathroom.

In a magnificent glittering gallery, hung with chandeliers and tapestries and furnished with brocade chairs, afternoon tea is served from silver pots while a pianist plays softly in the background; a wide choice of teas is offered to the *cognoscenti* in the Relais Plaza, accompanied by a harpist. The Régence restaurant, also famous for its musical Sunday lunches, is decked out with pink tablecloths and branched silver candelabra, portraits in oils and gilded plasterwork. I enjoyed sampling the crowning glory of its menu, a rich lobster soufflé, solicitously served by candlelight, amid magnificent flowers. The hotel spends more on its flowers than on electricity, and its employees outnumber the guests by two to one.

The total refurbishment of the hotel in recent years has been carried out under the ever-vigilant eye of Franco Cozzo, originally from Sicily, but here since 1962, and now Managing Director of all three Trusthouse Forte hotels in Paris. Deeply involved with every last detail, he is a perfectionist who never stops caring, the courtly ambassador of his luxuriously appointed palace hotel.

*In the creeper-clad courtyard (opposite) bright parasols shade diners. Above: the elegant and ornate staircase. Overleaf: the Relais Plaza grill room – ultra-fashionable meeting place of the Paris elite.*

---

HÔTEL PLAZA ATHÉNÉE, 25 avenue Montaigne, 75008 Paris. **Tel.** (1) 47 23 78 33. **Telex** 650 092. **Fax** (1) 47 20 20 70. **Owners** Trusthouse Forte. **Managing Director** Franco Cozzo. **Open** All year. **Rooms** 261 (incl. 42 suites), all with bathroom (incl. wall shower), direct-dial phone, TV (incl. English/German/Italian channels), radio (4 channels incl. BBC), minibar, airconditioning, valet/maid/room service, 24-hr. laundry/drycleaning. **Facilities** Gallery-drawing room serving afternoon tea, courtyard-garden with summer dining, 4 private reception rooms, 3 elevators, barbershop/ beauty salon, news/theater-ticket stand, Dow-Jones teleprinter, piano-bar, car rental/secretarial service/babysitting by arrangement. **Terms** Deluxe. **Credit cards** All major cards. **Closed parking** Valet parking by hotel for fee. **Nearest metro** Alma Marceau. **Local eating** Taillevent, Lasserre, Ramponneau, Duquesnoy, Les Princes (George V). **Local shopping** Avenue Montaigne high-fashion luxury boutiques. **Of local interest** Musée d'Orsay; The Louvre; exhibitions at Grand Palais; River Seine tours on *bateaux-mouches*.

## Tapestried comfort

Smallest of the three Trusthouse Forte hotels in Paris, La Trémoille is often chosen by guests who want neither the grandeur of the Plaza Athénée (*see* p. 69), nor the enormous size of the George V (*see* p. 75). It is named after one of France's most gallant Renaissance heros, Louis II, Sire de la Trémoille, a "parfit" but far from gentle knight, since he was a ferocious warrior and victor of many battles. Born in 1460, he pacified and fortified Normandy, dying in battle at the age of 65, while courageously defending his king.

The hotel is built on a corner, so that as you enter, the foyer is on your right, with a recessed reception desk, elevator, and a handsome staircase which rises up majestically between ornately worked banisters to a tapestried half-landing. On the left is a seating area with a black and white checkerboard marble floor and Louis XVI-style chairs. This leads into a small, intimate bar with carved antique paneling, and a pleasant little restaurant with starched white cloths, and orchids on the tables. Sensibly, given the very elaborate restaurants at the two larger hotels nearby, where guests here may sign their bills, there is a simple menu of traditional French fare – salads, pâtés, soups, omelettes, grills, and pastries – offered throughout the day for the convenience of guests arriving from abroad, though still formally presented with attentive service. I sampled a creditable steak and green salad, and fresh raspberry charlotte. An outdoor sidewalk section for the restaurant is currently being built.

Many very famous eating-places are close at hand, but if you are planning a gourmet tour of Michelin-starred chefs, ask the hotel to reserve a table for you at the establishments of your choice when you book your room, to avoid disappointment. The French take food extremely seriously – businessmen will argue heatedly over dinner about the exact seasoning for a sauce. Parisians enjoy eating at their leading restaurants, which explains why they are often fully booked a month in advance.

My room was paneled in pink brocade – each floor has a different color scheme based on pink, green, blue, etc. – and had an inner and outer door, as in a Cambridge University college. There was a small, sparklingly clean chandelier, gleaming white paintwork, a mirror-fronted closet, bedside radio console with English-language programs, a safe, a clock, and armchairs. A white voile cover was placed over the blanket when the bed was turned down. The marble-floored, tiled bathroom had an extremely efficient shower and commodious robe. When I ordered tea, it arrived promptly, with freshly sliced lemon and a silver strainer. Breakfast was excellent and generous. In winter the hotel is kept very warm, and in summer it is airconditioned and cool, both much appreciated by transatlantic visitors. There are several large and graciously furnished period suites with separate drawing rooms, and two elegant conference rooms.

I looked at many hotels in this area, but found few with the pleasant atmosphere, helpful staff, and well-equipped, well-maintained rooms possessed by La Trémoille.

*Opposite: the roomy foyer and paneled bar leading to the small restaurant. Above: one of the comfortable bedrooms.*

HÔTEL DE LA TRÉMOILLE, 14 rue de la Trémoille, 75008 Paris. **Tel.** (1) 47 23 34 20. **Telex** 640 344. **Fax** (1) 40 70 01 08. **Owners** Trusthouse Forte. **General Manager** Augustin Benetti. **Open** All year. **Rooms** 111 (incl. 14 suites), all with bathroom (incl. wall shower), direct-dial phone, TV (incl. foreign-language channels), radio (incl. BBC), mini-bar, airconditioning, room service, laundry/drycleaning. Portable FAX machines on request. **Facilities** Foyer-drawingroom, restaurant, bar, 2 conference rooms, elevator. **Restrictions** None. **Terms** Expensive–deluxe. **Credit cards** All major cards. **Closed parking** Rue François Ier. Valet parking service. **Nearest metro** Alma Marceau. **Local eating** Lasserre, Taillevent, Laurent, Chiberta, Lamazère. **Local shopping** Avenue Montaigne high-fashion luxury boutiques. **Of local interest** River Seine tours on *bateaux-mouches*; exhibitions at Grand Palais.

## A majestic treasure-house

Now restored to its full late 1920s magnificence, the George V, built in the great age of the transatlantic liners, has an enormous foyer designed comfortably to swallow up passengers arriving with huge mountains of cabin trunks. Its vastness dwarfs enormous flower arrangements and gigantic twin candelabra – but is softened by groups of inviting red velvet armchairs and a magnificent, specially made Savonnerie carpet which took two years to weave. An antique Louis XIV tapestry hangs behind the long reception desk on the left, and a giant carved eagle spreads its vast wings over the porters' desk on the right. The hotel is a treasure-house and even has a Renoir, though this is alas in safe storage.

Arriving guests are received swiftly, politely, and efficiently; many of the staff have been here for years – some up to thirty. Through twin arches are glimpsed deep blue carpets and sparkling boutiques edging the immense inner courtyard, which is filled in summer by flowers and crimson parasols. An anteroom, with the marble bust of a pensive *duchesse*, has on one side a Thirties-style bar, on the other a baronial-sized drawing room with deep velvet armchairs. Hidden away among the four miles of corridor are splendid private reception rooms, including one hung with Aubusson tapestries, containing Louis XIII furnishings, and a huge carved overmantel from a Loire château.

There are twenty-one different styles of room, ranging from my own modest single room – with a carved wooden bed, framed oil-painting of flowers, sprigged fabrics and pink bathroom with marvelously deluging shower – to sumptuous suites with four-poster beds and large private balconies. All are airconditioned, and almost all have been totally refurbished by owners Trusthouse Forte (check that yours has been when booking): size and grandeur of room dictate the price.

One eats exceptionally well at the George V. An abundant breakfast included miniature pain au chocolat, croissant, sweet roll, crunchy bread, madeleine, seven little pots of different conserves, plenty of butter, and excellent coffee, all served on pretty Limoges china. You may have a simply served light lunch or afternoon tea in the grill room: I sampled an artichoke heart salad, grilled turbot, and a meltingly light fresh strawberry tart from an appetizing selection offered on a trolley. The Michelin-starred Les Princes main restaurant must not be missed; try either the very good value businessman's lunch menu, or a leisurely dinner, when a pianist plays. I found the potato galette with duck liver pâté, gorgeously presented roasted sea bass with faintly orange-flavored sauce, well-chosen cheeses, and chocolate pistachio dessert absolutely outstanding. The decor is most agreeable, with blue flower-and-bird tapestry chairs. I doubt whether even in its early heyday one was more comfortable or better fed at the majestic George V.

*For all its vastness, the George V offers corners for quiet conversation (opposite, top), the intimacy of a softly lit bar (opposite, below), and outside dining in a flower-filled courtyard (above).*

HÔTEL GEORGE V, 31 avenue George V, 75008 Paris. **Tel.** (1) 47 23 54 00. **Telex** 650 082 (messages); 290 776 (reservations). **Fax** (1) 47 20 40 00. **Owners** Trusthouse Forte. **General Manager** Michel Bonnetot. **Open** All year. **Rooms** 292 (incl. 59 suites), all with bathroom (incl. wall shower), direct-dial phone, TV, radio, minibar, valet/maid/24-hr. room service, laundry/drycleaning. Possibility of private video. **Facilities** Drawing room, 2 restaurants, bar, courtyard-garden, 7 large and many small reception/conference rooms, 5 elevators, Nina Ricci/Cartier/Givenchy/George V boutiques, newsstand, car rental/babysitting/secretarial services/photographer by arrangement. **Restrictions** None. **Terms** Deluxe. **Credit cards** All major cards. **Closed parking** Valet parking by hotel for fee. **Nearest metro** George V. **Local eating** Taillevent, Lasserre, Ledoyen, Laurent, Marius et Janette, Chiberta, Jamin, Ramponneau, Fouquet's. **Local shopping** Avenue Montaigne high-fashion luxury boutiques. **Of local interest** Arc de Triomphe; River Seine tours on *bateaux-mouches*; cabarets Le Lido, Crazy Horse.

## Epitome of excellence

If you are bringing the Rolls to Paris, and want a central hotel with its own underground parking and porters who can be trusted not to mishandle the matched set of Vuitton, undoubtedly you will find the Hôtel Le Bristol to your taste. Probably the most exclusive hotel in town, like London's Connaught it has a faithful clientele who would not consider staying elsewhere in Paris, and who likewise patronize its sister establishments, the Eden Roc in Antibes, Brenner's Park Hotel in Baden-Baden, and the Park Hotel in Vitznau. In its time the Bristol has played host to many famous people, but it prefers the old-school diplomat or the stylish movie star to today's brash and noisy young pop idol. The loudest sound you are likely to hear in the marble halls of the Bristol is a gentle tinkling of teacups, ice-cubes, or piano, and a quiet murmur of conversation.

The extensive gardens, with arcaded walk and manicured lawns edged in clipped boxwood hedges, provide a vast green open space for guests. The foyer is scattered with handsome Persian rugs; the chandeliers are Baccarat crystal; and the furniture is genuinely antique, some pieces purchased from the Louvre in the Twenties by the hotel's original owner. The handsome oval winter restaurant is lined with carved wooden panels and tapestries; the summer restaurant is tented in striped awnings with huge glass windows opening onto a terrace and the gardens. Both restaurants are lavishly decorated and overflowing with fresh flowers.

Rooms in the Bristol's newer wing, La Résidence, built on the site of a former convent, all overlook the gardens. Slightly more modern in decor than the original rooms, like them they are filled with fine antiques, prints, oil-paintings, and chandeliers. The bathrooms are all superb – I would say the finest of any hotel in Paris – huge, in white marble, with vast shower stalls as well as tubs, illuminated make-up

mirrors, hot rails, big towels, and toiletries by Hermès. Room service is impeccable, and the hotel chef has a Michelin star; even the bartender has won prizes for his cocktails. The covered rooftop pool with sea-going murals and teak decks was conceived by the designer of the Onassis and Niarchos luxury yachts.

The initial greeting at the Bristol is exquisitely polite but not effusive – though returning guests are instantly greeted by name and all their preferences recalled. Arriving with an introduction from one of their established clientele helps to break the ice; the distinguished General Manager Monsieur Marcelin finds he is now welcoming to his completely and magnificently refurbished hotel many transatlantic and European guests whose grandparents always stayed at the Bristol in the Twenties. The tradition of excellence continues to be upheld.

*The luxury of a vast manicured green lawn in the exclusive hotel garden (opposite) and exquisite furniture (above) are just two of the riches of this magnificent hotel. Others include (overleaf) bedrooms with commodious mirrored closets; teatime on the terrace; and a charming period lift, run with modern efficiency.*

HÔTEL LE BRISTOL, 112 rue du Faubourg Saint-Honoré, 75008 Paris. **Tel.** (1) 42 66 91 45. **Telex** 280 961. **Fax** (1) 42 66 68 68. **Owners** Société Hôtel Jammet le Bristol (French and German shareholders). **Managing Director** Raymond Marcelin. **Open** All year. **Rooms** 200 (incl. 45 suites), all with bathroom (incl. stall shower), direct-dial phone, TV (incl. satellite channels), radio (incl. BBC), minibar, airconditioning, 24-hr. room service, in-house laundry/drycleaning. **Facilities** Bar/lounge with afternoon tea/drinks (also served outside in summer), pianist in evenings, summer restaurant April–October, winter res-taurant November–March, large formal garden, 4 elevators, babysitting/secretarial services by arrangement, beauty salon/barber shop, covered rooftop pool, solarium, sauna, 6 conference rooms. **Restrictions** No dogs. **Terms** Deluxe. **Credit cards** All major cards. **Closed parking** At hotel, free to guests. **Nearest metro** Miromesnil/ Champs-Elysées Clemenceau. **Local eating** Ledoyen, Laurent, Taillevent, Chiberta, La Marée. **Local shopping** Rue du Faubourg St.-Honoré boutiques, galleries, jewelers, furriers, shoe shops, perfumers. **Of local interest** Arc de Triomphe.

## Courteous formality

The Savoy group of London, which includes Claridge's, the Berkeley, and the Connaught, also own a small exclusive Paris hotel in the rue de Berri, bought in 1970. It is named after the city of Lancaster, whose arms appear on its letterhead. Built as a private residence in 1869 by a Monsieur Santiago Drake del Castillo, the Lancaster was sold in 1925 by his heirs, the Comte and Comtesse Ferrent, to a Swiss hotelier, Emile Wolf. He added a further four floors to the mansion, and filled it with a splendid collection of genuine and reproduction antiques, creating a highly idiosyncratic hotel which attracted the great personalities of the time: King Umberto of Italy, the Nizam of Hyderabad, Noel Coward, Clark Gable, Greta Garbo, and Marlene Dietrich – after whom a favorite suite was named.

Walk into the hotel today, down the long corridor which was once the carriage drive, and you emerge into the former courtyard, now a drawing room. A nostalgic echo of the past lingers on in the antique velvet chairs, the formal pyramids of glorious fresh flowers, the ornately painted clock reflected in a tall mirror, and the doors opening into a classically French courtyard – once the stables – which is green with hanging vines and ferns; here stand two life-size bronze deer, the work of François Pompon, accepted in settlement of the long-overdue account of a now long-vanished impecunious countess.

Purposely, no hovering presence or hospitality desk dispels the illusion that you have wandered into a private house or club, though the gleaming array of bottles behind the small bar in the inner room suggests a welcoming host. The reception and porters' desks are hidden away up two steps at the end of the drawing room – though if you have arrived with bags an elegant, Savoy-trained young man in black jacket and striped trousers, alerted by the porter at the door, will have hurried through to greet you, and will show you up to one of the gracious bedrooms, recently refurbished in either satins or chintzes. Most of the bathrooms are now modern – some, however, in answer to guests' pleas, have retained their original Thirties fittings and painted tiles. Rooms on the street side are airconditioned; those overlooking the inner courtyard are not, but are cool and quiet. Be specific about preferences when booking, enquire about special weekend breaks, and ask the hotel to reserve a table if you wish to dine at a famous nearby restaurant. Housekeeping has the inimitable Savoy polish – a well-ironed cotton cover was placed over the headboard when the fine linen sheets on my bed were turned down.

Do not come expecting a traditional English tea, as this is not served, though breakfast is ample and delicious, and there is a small restaurant for those resisting the temptation of the surrounding galaxy of Michelin-starred establishments. The Lancaster is a much-esteemed Paris *pied-à-terre* for those often-returning traditionalists who appreciate its period furniture and its unruffled calm.

*Savoy traditions continue in the beauty of the flower arrangements (opposite) and the grandeur of the bedrooms (above).*

HÔTEL LANCASTER, 7 rue de Berri, 75008 Paris. **Tel.** (1) 43 59 90 43. **Telex** 640 991 LOYNE. **Fax** (1) 42 89 22 71. **Owners** Savoy Group. **Director/General Manager** Roland Linhardt. **Open** All year. **Rooms** 66 (incl. 9 suites), all with bathroom (incl. wall shower), direct-dial phone, TV, radio, minibar, 24-hr. room service, same-day in-house laundry/pressing (except weekends and holidays), drycleaning. **Facilities** Drawing room, restaurant, bar, courtyard garden with summer dining, 2 private dining/ reception/conference rooms, elevator. **Restrictions** No dogs in restaurant. **Terms** Deluxe. Ask about special weekends/champagne breaks. **Credit cards** All major cards. **Closed parking** Opposite hotel. **Nearest metro** George V. **Local eating** Ledoyen, Laurent, Taillevent, Chiberta, La Marée. **Local shopping** Rue du Faubourg St.-Honoré boutiques, galleries, furriers, jewelers, shoe shops, perfumers. **Of local interest** Arc de Triomphe; Eiffel Tower.

## The best-kept secret in Paris

To say that the Balzac is a small hotel would be totally misleading – it is, rather, a smaller version of one of the grand turn-of-the-century Paris hotels, with staff, service, and comfort to match. It is named after the road on which it stands, in which the famous 19th-century French writer Honoré de Balzac once lived, a quiet backwater just off the Champs-Elysées.

The exterior of the hotel is discreet, with no large sign on display, though you can find it by the cheerful, geranium-filled windowboxes and elegant lanterns embellishing its stone façade. A flight of marble steps leads upwards from the corner entrance, and a smartly uniformed porter hurries down them to welcome and assist you. Above the porter's desk hangs a huge carved royal coat of arms – perhaps awarded by a frequent patron? A fine chandelier lights the broad foyer, which is decorated with giant sconces and a vast oil-painting of a sleeping Diana the Huntress. Tea may be taken in an inner atrium, which has been roofed over in darkened glass and has alcoves painted with landscapes.

Beside the entrance stairway is the way in to the Sallambier restaurant, named after the family name of Balzac's mother. The decor is palm court Thirties, as is the small, pleasant bar, with indirect lighting, peach-tinted engraved glass, and palm trees in pots. Tables are well-spaced; service is polite, attentive, friendly and very professional; and there is a choice of à la carte or an excellent set menu. Asparagus tips in puff pastry with a light sauce, a delicious grated potato and codfish confection with mushrooms and spinach, a selection of cheeses in excellent condition, and chocolate dessert with a hint of mint were memorable.

The hotel was recently gutted to its 1910 exterior walls and entirely rebuilt, which explains the large smoked-glass modern elevator and spacious modern bedrooms; these are airconditioned, with capacious closets and splendid marble bathroms supplied with Nina Ricci goodies. My bedroom had a six-foot bed, pretty reading lamps made from antique painted oil lamps, a wide desk, framed prints, and Suzy Langlois fabrics in a muted paisley pattern of reds, blues, and greens. One top-floor suite has a wide balcony with stunning views of the Eiffel Tower, and has a pink marble bathroom with a jacuzzi. The adjoining suite, with views over the terraced garden, has its own vast drawing room with a bar. A series of junior suites are less vast, but very attractively furnished.

Breakfast brings a succulent selection of breads, croissants, and pastries, with in-house *A l'Ancienne* conserves. Room service is swift, and when I requested a hairdrier, it was brought rapidly to my room by a well-groomed housekeeper. With its general air of well-organized quiet efficiency, well-trained, unobtrusive staff, and comfortable rooms, it is not surprising that this quiet hotel, the best-kept secret in Paris, should often be chosen for low-profile Paris trips by publicity-shunning royals.

*Opposite: a jazzy range of cocktails in the bar (below) precedes dinner in the art-deco-style, palm-filled restaurant (above). Modern comforts can be found in the bathroom. Above: a roomy suite with a wide, awning-covered balcony overlooking Paris.*

HÔTEL BALZAC, 6 rue Balzac, 75008 Paris. **Tel.** (1) 45 61 97 22. **Telex** 290 298. **Fax** (1) 42 25 24 82. **Owners** S.A. Celtic. **Managing Director** Christian Falcucci. **Open** All year. **Rooms** 70 (incl. 14 suites), all with bathroom (incl. wall shower), direct-dial phone, TV, radio, minibar, airconditioning, 24-hr. room service, laundry/drycleaning. **Facilities** Reception/seating area, covered atrium, restaurant, bar, private dining room with conference facilities, secretarial services by arrangement, terrace garden, elevator. **Restrictions** None. **Terms** Expensive–deluxe. **Credit cards** All major cards. **Closed parking** Champs-Elysées. Valet parking at hotel. **Nearest metro** George V. **Local eating** Taillevent, Chiberta, Ledoyen, Fouquet's, Laurent, Patrick Lenôtre, Guy Savoy, La Marée. **Local shopping** Rue du Faubourg St.-Honoré boutiques. **Of local interest** Arc de Triomphe; Eiffel Tower.

## Twenties sparkle

This hotel has some of the most spacious and comfortable bedrooms in Paris. Owned by Middle Eastern interests and affiliated to the Italian Ciga Hotels company, it is luxurious, conveniently sited, and highly sophisticated. It was built at the end of the 1920s when Josephine Baker and Maurice Chevalier were the up and coming young cabaret stars, and Coco Chanel was just getting into her stride as a designer. Braque and Dufy, Chagall, Matisse, Dali, and Picasso were in their prime; James Joyce and Ernest Hemingway could be spotted in sidewalk cafés, and Lalique crystal, complicated cocktails, and the Charleston were all the rage. Guests were exotic – Indian maharajahs with their scimitar-brandishing retinues, leading political figures, American multimillionaires, and international film stars.

Totally refurbished, the Royal Monceau has recaptured its glittering Twenties sparkle, and hums with life. The original fan-shaped porch of twirly cast-iron and glass shelters the graceful entry arch; the small, highly polished foyer neatly contains all the service desks in side arcades, and opens into a pillared hall. This has a gleaming checkerboard floor, a vast marble table with glorious fresh flowers, a cloud-patterned oval ceiling, a sedan chair, inviting velvet settees, mirrored walls concealing gracious reception rooms much in demand for select gatherings, and an elegant, tapestry-hung staircase.

A transparent covered walkway leads out to the carousel-shaped, glass-walled restaurant built over a spa complex and pool in the tree-lined garden. In fine weather you can eat outside under a parasol on the terrace; bad weather brings you under glass. Stuffed courgette flowers, slivers of four different types of fish in a subtle red-pepper sauce, and a pretty dessert of red summer fruits with a lemon and vodka sorbet were all excellent and served with great expertise. My meal was preceded by imaginative hors d'oeuvres and followed by a tiny tiered stand of miniature pâtisserie petits fours. I also enjoyed the hotel's Italian restaurant, decorated with green trelliswork, where delicious Mediterranean dishes are served by charming, well-trained staff.

My bedroom was large, with walls paneled in cream fabric with a tiny blue and yellow pattern, with matching bedcover, a whole wall of mirrored closets, an excellent bed, well-placed reading lights, two big armchairs, and a wide desk. The marble bathroom had gold faucets, soft towels, and robes. Breakfast, served on Bavarian china, was a delight. Maids in traditional black uniforms tidied the room whenever I went out, turned down the bed, and placed a linen foot mat beside it. I noted that I was requested not to leave anything valued at over 20,000 dollars in the room safe.

Demanding world travelers will find the Royal Monceau a most luxurious and satisfactory "home-from-home."

*Opposite: above, glittering foyer; below, light-filled, glass-walled restaurant; and (above) spacious, airconditioned comfort in the bedroom.*

HÔTEL ROYAL MONCEAU, 37 avenue Hoche, 75008 Paris. **Tel.** (1) 45 61 98 00. **Telex** 650 361. **Fax** (1) 45 63 28 93. **Affiliated to** Ciga Hotels. **Managing Director** Michel André Potier. **Open** All year. **Rooms** 219 (incl. 39 suites), all with bathroom (incl. wall shower), direct-dial phone, TV (incl. satellite English-language channels), radio, minibar, 24-hr. room service, laundry/drycleaning. **Facilities** Hall-drawingroom, 2 restaurants, bar, 7 reception rooms, garden with terrace, piano-bar, 3 elevators, pool and health club with café/sauna/gym/Turkish bath/beauty salon/barber shop. **Restrictions** No dogs in restaurants. **Terms** Expensive–deluxe. **Credit cards** All major cards. **Closed parking** At hotel. **Nearest metro** Charles de Gaulle/Etoile. **Local eating** Lasserre, Taillevent, Laurent, Ledoyen, Chiberta, La Marée. **Local shopping** Rue du Faubourg St.-Honoré boutiques. **Of local interest** Arc de Triomphe; Parc Monceau.

## An old-world ambience

For anyone who has been visiting France for many years, La Résidence du Bois will certainly bring back happy memories of staying in friends' houses furnished in the grand *vieille France* manner. It feels so much more like a private residence than a hotel that many guests treat it as their own Paris mansion, and return regularly each year, phoning ahead to confirm their arrival date just as one would to one's own housekeeper. Quite often they even forget to mention their name, but since Cécile Wingerter and her colleagues at the reception desk have been here for longer than they care to calculate, they generally recognize the voice.

Rooms come in all shapes and sizes, and are priced accordingly, from the small, plain and workmanlike, to a lavish suite with a wall of mirrored closets, oil paintings, sculpture, silk-covered antique chairs, and floor-length windows opening onto the quiet inner garden with its tall sheltering trees, grass, flowerbeds, and parasol-shaded tables. The entrance hall is lined with display cabinets of china, and throughout there are inlaid tables, Persian rugs, tapestries, candlesticks, plants, porcelain, ornately framed mirrors, and works of art filling every spare inch. The owners – not hoteliers but business people and keen art collectors – added extra treasures each year, until all available surfaces were covered. The small bar has a landscape mural painted by a noted artist, and some of the rooms have ceilings tented with fabric, in keeping, as is much of the period furniture, with the mid-19th-century, Napoleon III building, once the private residence of the Comte de Bonneaud. Ancient vaulted cellars reveal that a much earlier house once stood here.

The surrounding district is residential, exclusive, quiet and leafy, lying between the stylish avenue Foch, and the broad, tree-shaded avenue de la Grande Armée, which has many small cafés and

restaurants, and leads to the Arc de Triomphe and the Champs-Elysées. Guests who feel weary and decide not to go out to dine are served an elegant and delicious light meal, though the hotel will always book ahead a table at any of the surrounding Michelin-acclaimed restaurants, providing sufficient notice is given – that is, at least a month for the most fashionable.

If you want modern furniture and masses of uncluttered space, an imposing foyer, porters, boutiques, and an express check-out, this hotel is not for you. There is no Fax or Telex, and no credit cards of any sort are accepted. The Résidence du Bois, however, has its own unique personality and a great deal of civilized, old-world charm. Its many devotees often change their travel plans if their favorite room is not available, waiting until it is, since none of them would dream of staying anywhere else in Paris than at this patrician establishment.

*Guests can relax in the bar, with its unusual pavilioned ceiling (opposite, top); or in the quiet, grassy gardens. Shown above is one of the highly individual bedrooms of this patrician hotel.*

LA RÉSIDENCE DU BOIS, 16 rue Chalgrin, 75116 Paris. **Tel.** (1) 45 00 50 59. **Telex/Fax** None. **Telegraphic address** RESIBOISOTEL. **Owners** Family Desponts-Theocharides. **Manager** Mme. Theocharides-Desponts. **Open** All year. **Rooms** 19 (incl. 3 suites), all with bathroom (incl. hand or wall shower), direct-dial phone, TV, room service, laundry/drycleaning. **Facilities** Drawing room, sitting room, bar, garden with tables. NB No elevator, but several ground-floor rooms. **Restrictions** None. **Terms** Moderate–expensive. NB Breakfast included. **Credit cards** NB No credit cards accepted. **Closed parking** Place St.-Ferdinand. **Nearest metro** Argentine/Etoile. **Local eating** Patrick Lenôtre, Le Petit Bedon, Le Petit Colombier, La Coquille, Guy Savoy, Chiberta, Jamin, Faugeron, La Marée, Taillevent. **Local shopping** Rue du Faubourg St.-Honoré boutiques. **Of local interest** Arc de Triomphe.

## Exclusive grandeur

The Saint James's Club of Paris, with sister establishments in London, Los Angeles, and Antigua, was originally founded by jet-set entrepreneur Peter de Savary to provide demanding international travelers with an exclusive Paris base. Diplomats and concert pianists, film-stars and fashion designers enjoy its convenient location in a quietly fashionable area just off the Paris ring-road, convenient for nearby avenue Foch and Charles de Gaulle airport.

Driving in through the fine wrought-iron gates of this gracious turn-of-the-century mansion, you will find ample space to park. Uniformed porters whisk away your bags; urbane desk staff are welcoming and efficient. The lovely square hall soars up to a high balustraded gallery, and the majestic staircase is classified as a national treasure. An inner hallway has elevators and a second graceful staircase leading down to the gym, jacuzzi, and sauna – vital to those with high-pressure lifestyles – as well as a billiard room.

Seven of the bedrooms, some duplex, lead from a private rooftop wintergarden, with a sliding glass roof that can be opened to the stars. Thirties-style, bedrooms throughout have been designed with flair and a sympathetic understanding of a traveler's requirements – space, light, ample seating areas, king-size beds with sea-island cotton sheets, vast closets, and luxurious bathrooms with well-lit mirrors, wide surfaces for toiletries, robes, and plenty of generously sized towels. There is even a desk with terminal for personal computer and access to worldwide link-up. My studio room had an enormous entry hall, a well-stocked bar, indirect lighting, a brown sofa suitably shaped like a scallop shell – emblem of pilgrims to the shrine of St. James. Window blinds rose at the touch of a button, and a large oval coffee table did likewise and was then set out with a starched damask cloth and silver for meals.

I studied the luncheon menu sitting in the library, which has leather-bound books lining the walls up to the high ceiling, leather sofas in conversation groups, and a long bar at one end. Scallops in a light lobster sauce, a rack of lamb with tiny vegetables, and a fresh strawberry dessert were extremely good and served with style in the elegant restaurant under a cloud-painted ceiling, and with a view of the leafy gardens, where there is an outdoor summer dining area. You may take English afternoon tea in the library if you wish.

This is a private club, but daily temporary membership is available for a small fee – enquire for details – and your name can be put forward for full membership, which brings reciprocal rights in clubs worldwide, against annual dues, non-residents of Paris paying less. The Saint James's Club provides the comfort and privacy you would expect when staying in a friend's luxurious mansion, with the cuisine and service usually found only in a top hotel.

*This gracious mansion has its own flowery gardens and book-filled library bar (opposite). The restaurant (above) looks out into the trees. Overleaf: Thirties decor in a bedroom; a corner of the garden; the architecturally splendid hall and staircase.*

SAINT JAMES'S CLUB, 5 place du Chancelier-Adenauer, 75116 Paris. **Tel.** (1) 47 04 29 29. **Telex** 643 850. **Fax** (1) 45 53 00 53 00 61. **Owners** Norfolk Capital Hotels. **Manager** Kenneth Boone. **Open** All year. **Rooms** 48 (incl. 34 suites), all with bathroom (incl. stall showers), direct-dial phone, TV (incl. satellite English-language channels, videos on request), minibar, airconditioning, 24-hr. room service, same-day laundry/drycleaning (except Sunday), Transpac computer link. **Facilities** Drawing room, 2 restaurants with garden service in summer, library/bar, 2 reception rooms, billiard room, gym/jacuzzi/sauna with trained masseur/osteopath, garden, babysitting/cribs, 24-hr. film developing, baggage storage by arrangement. **Restrictions** Club for members or temporary members only. **Terms** Expensive–deluxe. **Credit cards** All major cards. **Closed parking** None, but ample parking in grounds. **Nearest metro** Porte Dauphine. **Local eating** Paul Chêne, La Grande Cascade, Orève, Jamin, Robuchon, Patrick Lenôtre, Giulio Rebellato, Le Pré-Catelan, Vivarois. **Local shopping** Many elegant boutiques in avenue Victor Hugo. **Of local interest** Bois de Boulogne; Longchamps racecourse.

## *Near the Palace of Versailles*

Those who wish to visit Paris in summertime but dislike the stifling heat that often grips the city should consider staying at the Trianon Palace Hotel, which is surrounded by cool and peaceful park-like grounds and lies on the edge of the gardens of the Palace of Versailles, nine miles outside Paris. Train or freeway take you swiftly into the capital, or on a day's outing to the soaring Gothic cathedral of Chartres, with its stained-glass windows, the forests and châteaux of Fontainebleau, or the Loire valley. The treasures of Versailles' richly elaborate rooms and wonderful formal gardens, with their fountains and alleys, clipped hedges and brilliant beds of flowers, merit several days' exploration; bicycles are provided by the hotel for the energetic.

The Trianon Palace Hotel was opened in 1911, the era of the great majestic hotels; it has fine gilded, wrought-iron gates, an imposing porticoed entrance, a long, arched chandelier-hung gallery, high-ceilinged reception rooms, broad terraces, and a palatial aspect. During World War I it was used as a British hospital, and in World War II it was first an RAF, then a Nazi, headquarters. As in the case of so many other splendid stately hotels, the fashion for concrete and glass modernity for a while led to a decline into shabbiness, from which, thanks to a growing appreciation for period charm, it has now triumphantly been rescued. Bedrooms, still with their vast built-in closets, tall windows opening onto the tree-filled gardens, fine marble mantelpieces, and large bathrooms – now modernized and tiled – are currently being restored; the attic rooms, which have panoramic views over fields of grazing cows and sheep, will be particularly charming. A spa with treatments for health and beauty has been added, together with a covered sunken pool, sunbathing deck, poolside bar, and restaurant; tennis courts were being constructed during my visit and are now ready for use. The staff are helpful and treat you with an old-world courtesy.

Weekends bring many wedding parties and family reunions, and on Sundays a resplendent buffet lunch is served, with beautifully prepared dishes, lobsters, roasts, and wonderful creamy desserts; in good weather you may eat out on the terrace. I enjoyed watching some elaborately dressed children playing happily among the groves of trees, returning to sit demurely and work their way with great gusto through a multi-course meal. On weekdays the reception rooms are filled with conferences and meetings – but there is still ample space for individual guests.

The Trianon Palace Hotel is traditional and majestic, a family resort hotel *par excellence*, returning rapidly to its former glory; a pleasant, leafy base for sightseeing in and around Paris.

*The hotel's imposing and richly ornate entrance (overleaf, left) leads into a polished marble hall, illuminated by a delicate crystal chandelier (opposite). Above: a mouthwatering fruit dessert. Overleaf, right: the vast, all-weather glass-roofed pool and extensive sundeck beyond.*

TRIANON PALACE HOTEL, 1 boulevard de la Reine, 78000 Versailles. **Tel.** (1) 39 50 34 12. **Telex** 698 863. **Fax** (1) 39 49 00 77. **Owners** Trianon Palace S.A. **Manager** J.P. Marcus. **Open** All year. **Rooms** 120 (incl. 10 suites), all with bathroom (incl. wall shower), direct-dial phone, TV (incl. satellite channels in English, German, and Italian), minibar, room service, same-day laundry/drycleaning/pressing (except weekends and holidays). **Facilities** Drawingroom-gallery with afternoon tea, restaurant, bar, 4 reception rooms, 2 elevators, bicycles free to guests, car rental, 2 tennis courts, health complex with covered pool, gym, 2 saunas, health and beauty treatments with balneo-therapy, massage, solarium, poolside restaurant and bar, extensive wooded gardens. **Restrictions** Dogs in bedrooms only. **Terms** Moderate–deluxe. Half-board, week-end terms/special breaks available. **Credit cards** All major cards. **Closed parking** None, but ample parking in grounds. **Nearest train station** 3 within ½ mile of hotel. **Local eating** Les Trois Marches, Rescatore, La Boule d'Or. **Local shopping** Many small local boutiques. **Of local interest** Versailles Palace and gardens; within day's drive: Chartres, St.-Germain-en-Laye; Fontainebleau; Loire valley.